To Danny & Marie

My very good friends
hope you enjoy !

George Salvester
17/4/2012.

MARIE'S
DANNY'S

It's the sailor, not the boat

George Selvester

"Smooth seas do not make skilful sailors."
African Proverb

-

Acknowledgements and Foreword

Recollections from my Royal Navy days are a little cloudy and my thanks to my mates from the *HMS Dunkirk Association* who prompted me in facts from those times.

Recollections of the years I spent at Blackness were from also gleaned from my memory and I have surprised myself at how much I could actually remember of the events and cruises.
However, I did have to call on some of my old sailing buddies from that time to help occasionally.
My thanks to: Donald Thomson, Joe McCrystal, Dan Markey, Tam Linton and Peter Robertson.
Some of the pictures from those years are thanks to a presentation album I was given when I left Blackness in 1993.
From 1993 onwards I started to record details in sailing logs and they are reproduced several times in the book.

I have no doubt that there may be slight discrepancies from the recollections of my early years, but on the whole they reflect my experiences.

George Selvester

"Selvester! You will never make a sailor as long as your arsehole is pointing to the ground!"

The words rang in my ears, as I tried to take in what the Petty Officer Instructor was telling me. This is my first recollection of sailing instruction at HMNB Jupiter Point in Cornwall.

At first, I felt rather intimidated by the comments of the instructor, in retrospect I realise he managed to give me something that would stay with me for the rest of my life!

In the '40s and '50s I had been brought up in the West Pilton district of Edinburgh and as a youngster I would go down to Granton to watch the yachts going in and out of the harbour thinking that one day I might be lucky enough to own one just like them.

Where it all started

In October of 1960, I entered *HMS Raleigh* to begin my Royal Navy basic training as a "junior stoker" it was at that time I experienced my first taste of the seamanship school.

After several heavy study days at classes, we would be given a "rest day", which involved being given a packed lunch, loaded into an RN Ford Thames 3 tonner canvas covered truck and taken to Jupiter Point, where we spent the day sailing "3in1" 27ft *Whalers* and 32 ft *Cutters*.

At 17 years of age at HMS Raleigh

These boats were traditional naval craft and referred to as "3in1" because of their ability to be "rowed" "sailed" or "motored". They were fitted with rowlocks and thwart seats and long oars for rowing, a mast step and a "drop" keel for sailing and an inboard engine for motoring with the traditional transom rudder serving as steerage for all forms of propulsion.

Initially I found it really hard work, the group first had to learn to row the craft which, to start , was very difficult but we all gained a great deal of satisfaction from learning to row in unison thus making it a lot easier to propel the boat in the desired direction at a fair lick of speed.

However sailing these boats was what fascinated me; I had never actually seen the use of proper sails, the nearest I had been to this was sailing the model yacht my uncle, John Pringle, had given me as a boy which I did on Inverleith pond in Edinburgh.

To see the real thing was wonderful and I found it difficult to comprehend how we could sail so close to the wind.

Using the motor was relatively boring, unless you were on the version with Kitchener Gear. To motor this boat was quite difficult, as it was propelled by a motor using what was known as the "Kitchen" Rudder, where buckets round the propeller could be adjusted to give forward or reverse motion to the boat and to steer it was an acquired art. See:

www.wikipedia.org/wiki/Kitchen_rudder.

To learn boat handling with such equipment has stood me in great stead ever since. It is always easy to put headway on rather that take it off, which is why to this day I always approach slowly rather than at speed, that way I can prevent the boat from "ramming" whatever I intend coming alongside.

Once we had mastered the art of sailing on the whalers and cutters, we graduated to more sophisticated sailing aboard the sailing dinghies, I cannot really remember what they were then but I am told by others that they were in fact the *RNSA* 14 ft Gaff rigged *Admiralty Designed Dinghies*. These would later to be replaced by the 14ft *"bosun"* in the mid 1960's. More information on this subject is available on the "Bosun" owners' website.

I was at Raleigh from 25th Oct 1960 to 23rd May 1961 After my basic training I was put into the draft "pool" awaiting my first sea going draft. I spent a lot of this time back down at Jupiter Point.

On 24th May 1961 I was transferred to *HMS Drake* at Devonport, to join *HMS Dunkirk*, a Battle Class Destroyer for her commission.

"Dunkirk" was a really good and happy ship. After we did our "work up" and "sea trials" at Portland we went off to exercises in the Atlantic and to show the flag calling into Bantry Bay in Ireland, Guernsey, in the Channel Islands then through the Kiel Canal visiting ports in the Baltic returning via the Kattegat and Skagerrak to Devonport in September.

HMS Dunkirk

In October 1961 *HMS Lion* was commissioned and was sent out on a world tour. *HMS Dunkirk* and *HMS Leopard*, a frigate, were deployed as the escort ships and we travelled around South America visiting Rio de Janeiro, Buenos Aires, Mar del Plata, Commodoro Rivadavia, Valparaiso, Callao, Cartagena, Panama, San Juan (Puerto Rico) and the Azores. When returning to Devonport we were diverted to the Mediterranean fleet to replace *HMS Broadsword*, (which had engine troubles) in the 7th destroyer squadron, based at Sliema Creek in Malta.

The ship had its own little sailing dinghy, a Piccolo, courtesy of the Nuffield Foundation.

4 stokers after "Divisions"
me centre (seated) 1962

When playing football in Malta, I collapsed with a serious asthma attack and was taken to Royal Naval Hospital, Bighi.

I returned to the Dunkirk shortly after that but was to be "CasEvac" (casualty evacuation) back to UK on 3rd December 1962.

On my return to UK on an RAF Comet, landing at RAF Lyneham, I was transferred to RNH Haslar at Gosport. After an assessment there, I was deemed fit to return to duties and was posted to *HMS Drake* awaiting another draft.

In May of 1963 I was then drafted back to *HMS Raleigh* as Ship's company, this again allowed me to visit Jupiter Point on a regular basis and enjoy my sailing. I recall sailing amongst the trots off Devonport seeing the "mothballed" fleet on the moorings.

My stay at Raleigh was short-lived (September 1963) and I was soon on my way to *HMS Sultan* in Gosport for Diesel courses. I specialised in Deltic Engines, these were used in the Minesweepers and were also the same engines used in the diesel electric trains.

On 12 November 1963 I was drafted to *HMS Lochinvar* at South Queensferry, now the site of Port Edgar Marina. This had a double bonus for me as it was a short trip on the bus to visit my folks at home in Edinburgh and the base had a Royal Naval Sailing Association with dinghies to sail. The time of year did not help as it turned out and I got very little time on the water.

1st March 1964 I was drafted to HM Dockyard Chatham, where I commissioned *HMS Chichester* and went all through the "work up" and sea trials once again. I found no time for sailing during this time and in June of 1964 I married my first wife Ellen, in Edinburgh.

HMS Chichester

January 1965 saw me being transferred back to RNH Haslar for further tests on my asthmatic problem and after 3 months of tests and assessment I was discharged as medically unfit for service. I was devastated! What the hell was I going to do now?

My first son, Steven was born in December 1965 and second, Stuart in April 1967. I now had responsibilities that would keep me away from sailing for quite a while.

After life in the forces, I found it very difficult to settle into civilian life and seemed to be in search of some kind of Utopia. I spent a couple of years in Edinburgh, and then moved to Coatbridge, from there I moved to the Dava Moor in the highlands, I could not have been further from the sea! After a short time there I then moved to Laggan Bridge, just south of Newtonmore.
All still a great distance from the sea without any sailing.

Back near water again.

In 1978 I moved to Livingston and could at last get on a boat again.

For a while I would hire or charter boats for holidays, but they were mostly motor boats as Ellen did not like the thought of sailing with young children and my job as a long distance lorry driver did not give me much time for sailing, although I did play football a lot for a local team and ran to keep fit as well as a couple of marathons for charity.

We had several holidays on the Norfolk Broads, all on 40ft power cruisers, although on the odd occasion I did get a little sailing done on my own.

In early 1980s I acquired a broken down old boat, a 17ft plywood *Lysander,* which I bought for a song and set about restoring it. It had a mast, but no boom or sails and I made my own boom and sails, gaff rigged, and although it did not look at all pretty, I could sail it.

As I replaced the entire coach roof and cabin sides using plywood packing cases that would have otherwise been thrown in the skip, I was already doing my bit for recycling!

I removed the old rotten parts carefully to use as templates and when I rebuilt it I made some modifications by adding a solid spray hood with windscreens.

As it was when I first saw it

I left the long distance driving job and started driving small vans for a local firm so I could have time to study Transport Management at West Lothian College of Further Education, finally gaining a CPC and entry to Institute of Transport Administration.

The finished job

I was fortunate enough to secure a job as Transport Supervisor with Unichem in Livingston and at last I could get access to sailing again.

I joined Blackness Boat Club and I spent a lot of time crewing on other boats, often with Jack Ferrier who had a 26 foot *Newbridge Venturer* called "*Virago*" which sailed very well and I longed for the time I could own a decent boat of my own, something a little better that the *Lysander*.

The lad from whom I bought the Lysander had been using it as motor boat for fishing and it had a huge 15 HP Yamaha petrol/kerosene outboard on the stern, which was way too big and powerful for the size of boat, but it sure got me into ports and out of trouble very quickly.

Being dual fuel, it had to be started with the fuel switch set to "petrol" and when it heated up switched over to "kerosene". Likewise, when stopping it had to be put back to "petrol" to allow the kerosene to burn off or it would be impossible to restart.

Some of the members at Blackness called it the "cloud maker", for once it was started, it would have a trail of blue smoke following it.

When I finally arrived at Blackness to launch the boat, a crowd of the members stood round and applauded as it hit the water and actually stayed afloat.

I had renamed her as "*Gess*" for **G**eorge, **E**llen, **S**teven, **S**tuart, and as a little bit of wordplay when anyone asked me the name of my boat, I would tell them "*Gess*!" They would often have several attempts before I explained the story.

When I bought the *Lysander*, there was a homemade dinghy with it, which those at the club nicknamed "the wardrobe", simply because that is exactly what it looked like. It was pretty much just a shapeless box made out of ¼ inch plywood. Thinking back, I was either extremely brave or extremely stupid to trust my life in such a flimsy little craft, however needs must when you are on a tight budget and it served its purpose of getting me to and from the mooring.
The *Lysander* itself was safe, if a little ugly, but I would often sail her down the firth with the tide and stay overnight in harbours like Dalgety Bay, Port Edgar or Aberdour. I had a lot of fun with it, but it was certainly very limited in terms of speed and manoeuvrability.

One afternoon my nephew, Reg Walters, and I in the *Lysander* and Eric Sutherland with his wife, Betty, in his *Express Pirate "Eliza Jane"* went for a sail around the firth, we ended up east of the bridges when the weather took a turn for the worse and very strong westerly winds got up. The only place to get shelter was in Inverkeithing Bay, so that's where we dropped anchor. In the shelter of the land we had a comfortable enough night and being an early riser, I was up with the dawn.

Eric's boat was maybe 20yds away, when he appeared on deck from the cabin. At this point I must explain that the *Express Pirate* had no toilet facilities aboard, we "Yotties" refer to this arrangement as "Bucket and Chuck it."
He then proceeded to tip the contents of a bucket over the side, looking up; he saw me watching him and shouted

"That's Betty got her teeth in now!"

Eric is one of those guys you meet once in a lifetime.

A proper yacht of my own

During the season of 1986 a great little boat came on the market, Joe McCrystal was buying a *Newbridge Navigator* and his 17½ ft *Silhouette* "*Naomi*" was up for sale. I already knew the boat and this was the opportunity to at last get a fibreglass boat, I thought it was great and I agreed to buy it and sold the *Lysander*.

I was now the owner-skipper of my own proper sailing yacht!

The Silhouette "Naomi" renamed "Sonsie"

Now I was the owner of a proper yacht, I decided I would go to the RYA night school and gain qualifications for Coastal Skipper/Yacht Master. I indicated my intentions to my mates at the club and they all agreed it was a good idea and a whole group of us enrolled for the classes. The courses would teach seamanship/Navigation/Collisions at Sea regulations, Lights, Shapes, Sounds/Weather forecasting. This eight-week course was followed by an examination, which gave you a certificate that you could produce when going for the practical exam after achieving the necessary amount of sea miles and watch keeping hours. This along with a First Aid certificate makes you a Yacht Master.

Above all I wanted to be a responsible sailor: there are far too many people who just buy a boat and venture out to sea with no idea whatsoever of how to navigate or what to do when something goes wrong.

I went everywhere with that little boat! It was not the fastest of craft but it was a safe little boat and I sailed the length and breadth of the Firth of Forth. Port Edgar, Cramond, Granton, Musselburgh, North Berwick, Dunbar, around the Isle of May, Anstruther, Pittenweem, Elie, Kirkcaldy, Aberdour, Dalgety Bay, North Queensferry, Limekilns and Charlestown. Although there were two bunks, the accommodation was very cramped, (You could only put your trousers on whilst lying down) nonetheless I enjoyed spending nights away on her.

I raced the boat in the club races and managed to come in last in almost every one. The trouble was that with the tides at Blackness, most of the boats would manage to finish just after high tide and I would have to battle the tide for a couple of hours just to manage to cross the line. On most occasions all the others were half drunk by the time I got back to the clubhouse.

I entered a regatta at Port Edgar one weekend and my son Steve was crewing for me. On one leg of the course he asked, *"Is that supposed to be like that?"* pointing to the port cap shroud, blowing in the wind. Fortunately being on a starboard tack the strain was on the other shroud; I gave Steve the helm and yelled, "Whatever you do, don't change tack!" I caught the loose cap shroud using the boat hook and reattached the bottle screw, tightening as it well as I could whilst sailing. We then abandoned the race and took down the sails and motored into the marina to check all the bottle screws. That incident taught me a valuable lesson; I now religiously tape all my tightened bottles screws on the rigging using self-amalgamating tape, covered with a final layer of insulating tape, that way they are less likely to work loose.

I owe a lot to Blackness Boat Club, for it was racing the Silhouette that honed my skills as a sailor. I did not realise this at the time, but when I moved up to a bigger boat, it became very apparent that the perseverance I showed on "*Sonsie*" to keep going, knowing that I would be the loser, was improving my skills.

Today I still recommend to new sailors, the way to get the best out of your boat is to take part in racing. See what others are doing and experiment with sail tweaking, study the tides and generally improve your skills on the water.

The cruising side of things was a lot better than the racing as far as speed, distance and social interaction were concerned, as I could set off ahead of the rest of the fleet and they would catch me before we reached our destination. That way, we could at least be more of a group. On cruises today in my home club, we operate a "buddy" system to keep the slower boats and less experienced skippers within sight of the main group. This makes it more interesting to the new sailors and they can discuss points and ask for advice on things they saw others doing during the trip. It also helps in the "pub" conversations at night.
A lot of experiences stay with you and make good stories to up and coming young sailors whenever you are in their company (or to include in any books you may write years later).

One trip I remember, Donald Thomson, left his own boat *"Mistral"*, a *Caprice,* to sail with me on *"Sonsie"* and we set sail for round the Isle of May, in company with another club member, Peter Robertson, sailing single handed, in his *Elizabethan* 23 *"Belle Amie"*.

When we were about halfway, on the 35 mile trip, Peter radioed to say he was very unwell and asked if one of us could transfer to his boat and sail whilst he lay down. It was agreed I would do the transfer and Donald edged my boat *"Sonsie"* toward the stern of Peter's Boat, I was on the foredeck and as we approached with the boats heaving up and down I managed to step from one to other without mishap.

"Belle Amie" and "Sonsie" prepare to sail

Peter went below to lie down and I sailed his boat heading for Isle of May. The weather at that time was around a force 4 from the west, which made for really good sailing as we were on a run and making excellent time.

By the time we actually reached the Isle of May, I had to call for assistance from Peter to take a reef in both the main and the foresail.

The wind, which had been steadily rising all day, was now blowing at around force 7. We were fine with the reefs in, but Donald, a good bit behind us was having great difficulty in getting a reef in and had opted, instead, for spilling the sails. We were now to the east of the island and although we had a bit of lee, the wind was unmerciful on Donald in my little boat, he was sailing it like a dinghy!

At times I really thought he was going to be swamped but there was nothing we could do to help him in the conditions.

The journey from the island to Anstruther is only about 5 miles, yet it took us almost two hours to complete.

Once inside the harbour we were fine and after securing the boats we retired to the local hostelry to relive the journey and congratulate each other for coming through the experience unscathed.

Sailing is like that, you learn something every time you go out and you often get a fright from the sea to remind you who is in charge!

The return trip the next morning Peter asked Donald if he would crew with him leaving me to sail single-handed on the return journey. The weather was a little kinder than it had been the previous day but was still a bit more brisk that we would have liked at the top end of a force 5 and still from the West, which meant it was on the nose all the way home.

We set off at 0600 in the morning stemming the last of the outgoing tide and in an hour or so it would turn in our favour. Within the first hour the *"Belle Amie"* disappeared over the horizon and although they spoke to me via the VHF at first, after a while all went quiet and I felt very much alone out there.

At about 1300 I heard them calling on the radio again, telling me they were at anchor taking a little bit of shelter in the lee of Kinghorn Ness. It took me about another hour to reach them, Donald said that if I could get close enough he would rejoin me and let Peter continue single handed as he intended sailing all the way home, Donald and I could afford to make an overnight stop somewhere.

Donald duly joined me and I had a quick bite to eat as Peter disappeared round the headland of Kinghorn Ness. As soon as I had eaten something, Donald set about putting the sails up and in his enthusiasm put too much exertion on the jib halyard and tore the head out of the sail which immediately went slack and started sliding down the forestay. Donald said, *"No problem, we will just put the other*

jib up. "I asked, *"What will we use for a halyard?"*
Donald's reply was quite succinct. *"Shit."*
There we were, now with no headsail! It would be almost impossible to sail to windward without it.

To attempt getting to the top of the mast in the waves we were now experiencing would have been foolhardy. It was then that we came up with the bright idea that if we beached her on the still rising tide we could, if we hurried, pull one of us up to the top of the mast using the main halyard and retrieve the end of the jib halyard.
We had little time to achieve this as it was now approaching the top of the tide.
As we were executing this tricky manoeuvre we managed to draw a group of three or four spectators on the beach, wondering what the hell we were up to.
We did manage to get a hold of it and bring it down to deck level fitting a smaller jib to complete the journey as far as Aberdour for an overnight stay.
The trip home from there the following morning back to Blackness was uneventful in very good sailing winds.

The season after I acquired *"Sonsie"* we launched in early April and along with Joe and Annette in their *Newbridge Navigator, "Midnight Blue",* we went for a weekend cruise. We opted for a simple and short one to Port Edgar, which was only 5 miles from

Blackness. The trip took longer than we expected, for although we had the tide in our favour it was a bitterly cold easterly wind that was blowing and on top of that it was snowing. That is what you call dedication!

We moored against the pontoons and decided we would eat out at one of the local pubs, there are six in South Queensferry, off we went, settling for the nearest which is the "Moorings" and went inside for the warmth and the good food. We stayed there until it closed and made our way back to the boats in arctic conditions.

Despite the cold atmosphere in the boat, I drifted off to sleep quite quickly. When I awoke in the morning, there was a red glow inside the cabin. It was my nose! I quickly lit the little gas stove, not for a cup of tea, but simply to warm up the inside of the boat. We vowed we would never sail in those conditions again if we could avoid it.

In **1987**, during the summer of the season, the club had an open day in July and a lot of people came down to our "Try a Sail" event. One such person was Tam Linton, who became my regular crew until he found a boat the same as *"Sonsie"*, which he purchased. It was fairly run down when he got it, but he worked very hard over the winter months to have it ready for the following season and it looked great with all its polished brasses and varnished woodwork, shining like a new shilling. Tam renamed her *"Tarka"* after the otter.

The club had suddenly increased its membership and it seemed to attract many good sailors, all around the same age bracket, with several of us serving on the committee it soon became a very successful club in both social activities and sailing prowess.

The names I remember from that time are Donald Thomson, Tam Linton, Joe McCrystal, Dan Markey, Jim McCain, Jack Young, Peter Robertson, John Armstrong, Andy Wallace, George Callaghan, Jack Ferrier, Bob Black, John Farrington, Eric Sutherland, Scott McConnachie and John Carson, if there are any whose names I have forgotten, I am sure they will forgive me.

There was a healthy racing fraternity at the club and we would be out most weeks and in most weathers.

In one particular race in the midweek series:

Weather or not?

This is the story of a Tuesday night bleak,
Of a race in the series, held during mid-week;
Eleventh July was the advertised date
But instead of seven-thirty, we started at eight.
The tide it was low (only four point six)
The weather was funny, a bit of a mix.
One minute quite bright, with glorious sun,
Then the next minute, windy with clouds on the run.

There weren't too many who were willing to race,
Just the intrepid, in search of a place.
Ellen & Liz both did the O/D
Then along came **Dan Markey** to take it to three.
The total boats entered amounted to four,
A fearless crowd led by "El Commodore",
A **Navigator, Caprice** and two **Silhouettes**
Were preparing to race and were placing their bets.

The first one to fail was **George Selvester,**
Held on his mooring by the rising Nor'Wester.
Then **Joe and Annette** who were ready to start,
Saw the wind getting up and had change of Heart.
It was then that **Tom Linton** appeared in the bay,
And scuppered his chances in a spectacular way.
He came racing in on a very broad reach,
Failed to come about and went up on the beach.
With all boats abandoned, excepting for one
Who had started the race just after the gun,
The wind was still rising, and by now was quite brisk,
The solitary yacht was at considerable risk.
The rest of the crews, who had thrown in the towel,
Sat in the clubhouse, as the wind it did howl.
Laughing and joking and merrily drinking
Whilst **Donald** and **Peter** were in danger of sinking.

When in burst **Mike Smith** who was looking quite ill,
He had seen the position from his house on the hill,
Saying "I'm really quite worried, can they stay afloat
Until we can get out there with the club rescue boat?"
To allay Mike Smith's fears, we said, "Please do not worry"

Then we finished our drinks (there was no need to hurry)
It's not that we're heartless, or that we don't care,
But Donald and Peter are a resolute pair.

Then by hoisting a storm jib, they proved us all right,
And headed toward us (what a heart-warming sight)
We still launched the rescue at Mike Smith's insistence
But they managed all right without any assistance.
With humour and verse I've made light of this tale
But please do remember whenever you sail,
The sea doesn't act as you always expect
*It can be quite awesome, so **SHOW IT RESPECT!***

George Selvester

I sent this into the *Silhouette Owners' Association*
and they published it.

Although we were restricted by the tide, as we were
all moored on drying out moorings, we seemed to
have it off to a fine art. Needless to say all of the
boats in the club were bilge or twin-keel boats,
having to take the ground in between tides.

At this point, I still was last (even on handicap) in
club races and I complained that my handicap must
be wrong. This was greeted with *"**It's the sailor,
not the boat!**"*

The first real cruise.

I mentioned Peter Robertson earlier. At one stage Peter wanted to go to Holy Island for a cruise and as at the last minute his crew let him down, he asked if I would go as his crew. I talked it over with Ellen, my wife, and we agreed that I should go, as the experience would be good for me. Some other members of the club tried to talk me out of it by saying that Peter and I, being two entirely different characters, would fall out within the first few days and would spend a miserable trip together, locked up in a boat with nowhere to hide.

As it turned out we had a very enjoyable cruise and although it was true that we did get on each other's nerves a couple of times, our different skills complemented each other.

Although I did not keep a log of the cruise (I did not start to do this until after 1993) I do recall many events of the trip.

As Peter kept his boat at Port Edgar he picked me up by car and we set off from there, the trip down was pretty uneventful, I do remember we stopped at Dunbar and had a good meal in one of the local pubs, but not much else happened worth noting, we were tired after the 40 mile trip and retired to our sleeping bags early.

The following day we set sail fairly early and made the 35-mile hop from Dunbar to Lindisfarne. Having made our breakfast with cooking oil that was way out of date, we were both of us sick as dogs on the way down. The wind was rising all the time and by the time we were off Berwick upon Tweed, it had risen to over force 6.

The forecast had been for lighter winds than were experiencing at that time, so we did not worry too much, however before we reached Holy Island, the wind had increased even more and we were very relieved to be able to pick up a mooring in the lee of the island, just beneath the tower.

We got the dinghy out and inflated it so that we could row ashore; it was around 1400 when we actually landed. Hiding the dinghy under a convenient bush, we took a walk up to the town and visited the old priory where they make the famous mead. As you can enjoy a free sample before entering the priory, we did this three times before they sussed us out!

After a couple of pints in the local hotel, we decided to return to the boat only to find that the dinghy had sprung a leak in one of the tubes and was only half inflated, as we had not brought a pump ashore with us, we had no option but to row it back that way. This was a very precarious operation, which proved to be fine, until Peter alighted onto the boat and the dinghy with my weight in the centre, folded in half soaking me completely.

After changing into some dry clothes and having a bite to eat, we decided to move the boat into what serves as a harbour. It is no more than a jetty that dries out to expose a layer of thick mud, which the locals describe as "The Ouse". With Peter's boat being a drop keel, we lifted the keel so that she could take the bottom, secured all the ropes and made our way back to the pub.

We returned later to find that the water had receded, leaving us high and dry but we had left a little too much scope on the lines and she was lying over at a very steep angle away from the jetty. I rigged a pulley system using knots I had learned from driving long distance (the "carters hitch") securing ropes fore and aft and round the mast foot we adjusted one at a time and we managed to pull her back up to a position comfortable enough for us to get some sleep, when the tide came back in the boat righted itself completely giving us a fair night's sleep and the ropes kept her upright when the tide receded again. We stayed a couple of days in Lindisfarne, visiting some of the historical sites but any longer than that is a waste of time, in my opinion. We were preparing to leave on the tide next day, the forecast was not brilliant but we figured we could cope, as soon as we were afloat we cast off and made the passage back through the hazards to the open sea.

I am not sure of the distance we had achieved when it became absolutely dreadful. I had gone forward to rig a storm jib and together we took two slab reefs in on the main and yet we were still "slamming" into a northeast wind. At one point the spindrift was so painful on my eyeballs when trying to see where we were going, I wanted to cry out in pain.

Above the roar of the storm Peter yelled to me "*I have half a mind to turn back*!" I yelled back "*I have half a mind to agree with you!*" and turn back we did.

Once back through the hazards we again made straight for the Ouse and tied up alongside the jetty. Another yacht, a *Trintella* 30+, had been sitting on a mooring as we came back in, then appeared astern of us.

Peter and I went back to the pub. Pete was in a bit of a "strop" (bad mood) for having had to turn back and sat at a different table to me.

I tried to ignore his mood, knowing he would come out of it eventually.

Two very good looking women then entered the bar, ordered drinks and sat at the table opposite me, they could see that I was a sailor because I was still wearing my "Mustos" they then asked if I had just come into the harbour in the last hour. I said yes that was the case, they told me that they had followed our boat into the "Ouse" and that they were having problems as their dinghy had upturned in the storm whilst sitting on the mooring and submerged their outboard motor.

As Peter suddenly realised I was talking to two very attractive Dutch women, he became talkative again and moved over to my table, after a few minutes we managed to determine that the outboard they had was an old "Seagull", which are virtually indestructible. We agreed to go aboard their vessel and sort out the outboard.

Together Peter and I flushed the whole outboard with a fresh water hose then started to strip plugs etc to spray with WD40, as I felt it was a one man job, I joined the two girls below on their beautiful boat for a few drams of "Geneva Gin"

A few minutes later I heard the outboard roar into life and realised Peter had completed the job. We spent the rest of the night talking about boats in general; they informed us that they shared their boat. I observed the fact that I did not think boat sharing was a feasible option as the chances of falling out were quite high; one of the girls asked me "*Would you not share with your wife*"?

It was at that point I realised they were gay. We enjoyed their company for the rest of the night.

The following morning, the wind had abated slightly and we set off again as soon as we had enough water. We figured we could make it back to Dunbar and at least we would be back into the Firth of Forth and a step closer to home.

The trip as far as St Abb's head was pretty straight forward, although we were beating into the wind, which was coming from the northwest. As we headed into the firth on a more westerly course again, the wind started to pick up to a strong breeze, force 6.

Not willing to be caught out again, we reefed early and as we approached Torness, I could see ahead of us a yawl rigged day boat with full sails heading in the same direction as us. They were making good headway but it must have been hard going, as they would occasionally "round up" to the wind, an obvious indication that she was carrying too much canvas. Torness is about 5 miles east of Dunbar, our planned destination, and I was quite worried about their predicament; Peter, in his usual matter of fact way said, "*They will be fine*". We soon overhauled her as we were sailing very well with our reefs in and before long she was well astern of us, still "rounding up" but making headway.

The entrance into Dunbar harbour is a very confusing your first time; you <u>must</u> follow the directions in the almanac, despite the fact your eyes and heart will tell you "This is all wrong!" As you follow the leading line into the harbour, it is easy to convince yourself you are heading for a rock-filled dead end.

You are completely surrounded by rocks, and it is not until you are well inside the approach, that you see the entrance to the harbour.

Once we were inside and secured alongside, I went up onto the breakwater to see if that day boat we passed had made it to here, there was no sign of it!

As I climbed back down onto the harbour wall, I saw them coming through the harbour entrance.

We beckoned them to tie alongside us, as the fishermen of Dunbar do not like "Yotties" alongside them, and we had a refreshing conversation. They were a father-and-son sailing duo and as the father said,

"Taking in a reef involves Roderick hanging over the stern, something he dislikes doing, so we just left all sails up!"

Peter and I walked to the town to get some provisions from the local Co-op shop and stopped a pint on the way back down to the boat. We did not see them again until during the night.

After our meal we went for another walk and a nightcap before turning in. It must have been about two o'clock in the morning when Peter woke me saying, *"The wind has changed and the boats are taking a battering against the harbour wall, we will have to shift them"*

I jumped up and we both went out into the cockpit, wearing only our underpants.

The wind had indeed changed and brought with it driving rain. Peter knocked on the side of the day boat, which had a canvas cover draped over the boom to give the occupants some cover from the weather. From under this canvas appeared the father wearing pyjamas!

We explained the situation, saying we would have to shift the boats. The father nodded in agreement then said,

"*I'd better go and change*" and slipped back under the canvas.

I asked, "*What is he going to change into?*"

Peter replied "*Probably a dinner suit!*"

After shifting the boats to a better berth and drying ourselves off, we returned to the warmth of our sleeping bags.

The next morning the wind was still howling and was now blowing directly from the west, so would be right on our nose for the homeward trip. Peter decided to wait it out to see if it would abate by the afternoon, even though this meant we would lose the tidal advantage.

By mid afternoon it had dropped slightly, but was still going to be hard going. Peter made the decision to press ahead and if need be, we would sail into the night to get home. We set off in a force 5 westerly and prepared ourselves for a long haul; however it took a lot longer than we expected.

Peter decided, as skipper, that we would do 3-hour watches on the helm and head straight for Port Edgar. The sail at first was not too bad, as we were heading more or less WNW and it was not quite a beat, but as soon as we were level with Bass Rock, we had to come round onto a direct westerly course, right into the teeth of the wind, where it became really energy sapping. Although we were achieving a steady 5 knots of headway over the water, the tide had now turned against us and with our tacking, the "speed made good" over our rhumb line, was only around 2 knots.

At one point I had come on deck to take over my stint at the helm and asked, "*Where are we*?" "*Just off Cockenzie power station*" replied Peter. He then went below for a sleep. Exactly three hours later he emerged from the cabin asking, "*Where are we?*" and I replied "*just off Cockenzie power station*". Our position had changed quite a bit in those three hours, but by focusing on a single reference point like that, it seems as though you are never getting away from it. The tide was back in our favour and we could make better headway than we had done for the previous six or seven hours.

We suffered a similar effect approaching Inchkeith Island, which is a big lump of rock in the middle of the Firth of Forth. Although it was only five miles as the crow flies, it too never seemed to get any closer and when we finally reached it, it never seemed to go away!

Darkness was falling as we approached Inchkeith and we shortened our watches, taking turns of the navigation and chart work. Sailing by day in familiar waters is much easier, as most things are readily recognised in broad daylight, but having to identify everything by its light characteristics is a lot more difficult. We were now coming into the narrower part of the firth and the scatter of lights from the shore exacerbated the problem of identifying lights and markers. It was also the most hazardous, with lots of unlit obstacles like *Inchmickery*, a small unlit island and the *Cow and Calves,* a group of three rocks just to the north of that island

Once we had passed the Herwit starboard hand buoy, just south of Inchkeith we held our westerly course until level with the west Cardinal mark for middle bank then headed NW for Oxcars light keeping the white sector light in our view, if we had gone into the red sector we would be standing into danger from the hazards mentioned.

Once reaching Oxcars Light we were in the main Channel to pass under the bridges.

We completed the whole trip without further incident and berthed the boat in Port Edgar Marina just as daylight was beginning to return, we collected Peter's car and made our way home, tired and hungry but satisfied we had achieved our objective.

Loch Lomond

I tried to encourage my wife, Ellen to sail with me; she did come with me a couple of times, but was basically afraid of the sea.

An old friend of mine, Tom Jordan, who kept his motor cruiser "*Tomara*" on Loch Lomond, suggested that Ellen might like sailing there.

I put this to Ellen and she was keen on the idea so I booked a week off work and made plans for the trip.

Ellen and I went down to Blackness on the Friday night, hitched the trailer onto my car, an Audi 80, and recovered the boat from the water via the ramp. I dropped the mast, secured everything for the road and parked the trailer and boat alongside the veranda of the clubhouse so that we could climb into the boat to sleep for the night and set off first thing in the morning. We then joined some of the members in the bar for a convivial evening.

The journey to Balloch was easy and problem free, on arrival at the Balloch Marina and shop I paid for the use of the ramp, launched "*Sonsie*" raising the mast again and once I was happy with the rigging, I put the sails on and motored out of the river into Loch Lomond. That was where I made my first mistake. I had a chart, of sorts, of the Loch but it was not too detailed and with no local knowledge, I turned away from the channel too early and ran aground on a sandbank, this was in full view of one of the big motor boats that ply their trade taking tourists round the Loch.

Some of the "punters" on board began making derogatory remarks, in their Glaswegian accents, on my ability as a sailor; this was liked a red rag to a bull. There were some choice words exchanged and I am sure if I could have reached them, there would have been blood spilled.

The boat motored off leaving me to my problem of getting off the sandbank. The outboard did not have enough power to take it off and I tried "kedging" it off with an anchor still no luck. I was towing my rubber dinghy behind the boat so Ellen and I got into the dinghy to lighten the boat and we managed to move it then.

Back on board when afloat, we headed for about seven miles up the Loch to Luss, as Tom kept his boat on a mooring just round the bay from there. We joined them that night for a barbeque and a few drinks and made plans for sailing around the Loch for a few days following Tom and his wife in *"Tomara"*. The first few days were perfect as we found some terrific little coves and islands to go ashore and have picnics. Everything was pretty idyllic, but on the day before we were due to return, we were heading for the island of *Inchmurrin* where Tom had offered to buy us lunch at the restaurant there.

We were about a mile from the island. sailing in quite a brisk breeze, when we were suddenly hit by a big gust and the boat heeled well over. I wanted to take a reef in but Ellen was of no use to me at all and she had got such a fright when we heeled, that she just froze. I moored up alongside the jetty on my own, with Ellen completely silent.

Tom did buy us our dinner but Ellen sat very quietly throughout and when we were walking back down to the boat she demanded we make straight for Balloch again and get the hell off this water, I felt I was left with no option and bade Tom and his wife farewell before motoring the couple of miles back to Balloch.

I recovered the boat again onto its trailer, dropped the mast, secured for the road and we made our way home again to Blackness. As far as I can remember, that was the last time Ellen ever set foot on the boat.

Return to Holy Island

In June of 1989 the club agreed to do the Holy Island cruise, I intended going with *"Sonsie"* but the week before the cruise, Dan Markey approached me to ask if I would crew him on his boat *"Fat Sam"* a *Sunray 21*. At first I was a bit reluctant because I wanted to go with my own boat and with my son,

Steve, as crew. Dan insisted that there was plenty of room for the three of us aboard his boat and convinced me it was the right thing to do. I asked Steve what he thought and he agreed to go with Dan.

Donald Thomson was going with his new boat, a *Vivacity 20 "Play Misty"* with his son Christopher and Eric Sutherland as crew. As we had all agreed to do a night sail to log hours for night sailing for our Yacht Master certificates, we were due to set off at 2200 and Dan said he would meet us down at the Port Edgar Marina just after 2130.

Just after 2200 Dan walked into "The Moorings" pub in Queensferry to pull the five of us out. We all made our way down to the boats just as darkness was coming down; by the time we left at 2300 it was dark. Dan had already worked out the passage plan and we set the course in accordance with this. Just before we reached Oxcars light I looked astern and could see the navigation lights of a large ship heading our way. As we were in the middle of the main channel I suggested we move to port to allow the vessel to pass. Both Steve and Dan said that they could not see the lights, always difficult against the scatter of lights from shore, and decided not to move over. The VHF radio on the boat which was on "dual watch" on 16, the calling channel, and 74, the port authority channel, suddenly burst into life "*Port Control this is the ship ********, there is a pleasure craft ahead of us in mid-channel*" I quickly called port control to inform them that the pleasure craft was us and that we were now moving out of the channel.

We sailed through the night and as we passed St Abb's Head Coastal station, in the early morning,(0530) the weather forecast was being broadcast on the VHF. After the forecast there is the report from the coastal stations.

St Abbs head: weather fair, sea state "slight", I remarked that they could not have got out of bed to look and must have asked the milkman, as we were being tossed around like corks.

We arrived at Lindisfarne around lunchtime and as we sailed toward the marker buoy for the start of the leading lines over the sandbar, I looked behind and saw that Donald's boat had turned to starboard and was heading directly toward the moorings. I asked Steve to call Donald on the VHF and tell him "*the seagulls you can see ahead of you are paddling!*" They quickly turned to port again and followed us.

Not a great deal of note happened on the cruise. On the return journey we called into Dunbar for an overnight. The following morning there was absolutely no wind and the two boats motored out of the harbour and sat drifting, waiting for wind to get up. The boats were around 20 yards apart and the water was flat calm, when a seal popped up between the two boats. It swam around looking at us in turn before submerging again. Steve (who at that time was working at Edinburgh Zoo) started slapping the side of the boat, Eric who on the other boat asked

"*What the hell are you doing*" Steve replied "*trying to get it to surface again*"
"*That won't get it to surface*" replied Eric, Steve said, "*Well, it works at the zoo!*"
Eric: "Really? C*an it get me some tickets?*"
Steve said, "*Shut it, you baldy git!*"
Eric came back with "*I don't mind being bald, and I refuse to wear a toupee, it's like those guys with wooden legs... who are they trying to kid?*"

The wind came up about an hour later and we had a very good sail back to Aberdour where we met up with Joe McCrystal and his wife Annette in their *Newbridge Navigator "Midnight Blue"*.

Eric "jumped ship" at Aberdour, with the lame excuse that he had get home to cut the hedges, leaving Christopher as the only crew.
The following morning, the weather was bad and we discussed whether or not we should go, Donald motored out, put up his sails then radioed the others "*Don't come out here, it's crap!*" sailed back in and we stayed another night. '

Over the duration of the cruise, I was so impressed with "*Fat Sam*" I said to Dan that if he ever thought of selling I would like the first refusal. He agreed.

The Newhaven Incident

At the end of that month 24th June 1989 Donald and I were on a mini cruise, He was on his boat and I was on "*Sonsie*" on the Saturday morning we sailed the 11 miles down to Newhaven harbour in Edinburgh spent a pleasant lunchtime in the Peacock hotel. We decided to stay long enough to have a couple of pints and watch the under-16 youth football tournament final between Saudi Arabia and Scotland, which kicked off at 1500.

The game went to extra time so we bought another pint. It then went to penalties, so we bought another pint. Saudi won on penalties and we were now late so rushed down to the harbour and cast off to get going.

As we sailed toward the bridges on a beat, Donald went to the south of *Inchmickery* and I opted for the north side. I was about level with the island when I was in the middle of a tack and the boat was caught by a sudden gust of wind that knocked the boat right over I was already off balance and this threw me over the side. I still had the jib sheet wrapped round my right hand and found myself being towed along by the boat on a port tack. I was being dragged through the water at around three knots. I tried to get hold of the boat with my left hand but with the wet fibreglass of the boat my grip kept slipping. I thought that the jib sheet was the only thing between me and death!

I tried and tried to get a grip and eventually got a grip on the cleat on the Starboard quarter, feeling confident I had a grip on the boat, I let go the jib sheet. The boat stopped. My weight on the sheet had kept the shape of the sail and as soon as I let go, the sail it stopped drawing and it rounded up to windward and stopped.

I did struggle to climb up over the outboard motor; I was cold, I was wet and I was exhausted. Once aboard I sat shivering, then I thought "DO SOMETHING".

In my confused state of mind I figured that best thing to do was sail the three miles plus back to Newhaven for the safety of the harbour.

I don't recall tying up, I don't recall changing into dry clothes and the first thing I do remember was ordering fish and chips in the Peacock Hotel and paying for the meal with wet banknotes.

Donald who had obviously seen nothing of what had happened; the island had been between us and he simply thought that I had lagged behind somewhat. It was not until he was almost back to Blackness, with still no sign of me that he thought that something might be wrong and raised the alarm.

After my fish and chips I felt totally drained and went right back to the boat and into my sleeping bag and fell asleep immediately.

The following morning I thought I had better phone home before sailing back up the firth to Blackness.

It was then I was told that the Coastguard had been looking for me all night!

I was suitably embarrassed when I phoned the Coastguard to tell them I was alive and well. I took some stick from the club members for that escapade for a very long time.

I have no recollection of sailing the boat back to Blackness and although I was not really willing to admit at the time the experience had shaken me up, I had just had the biggest fright of my life.

Several weeks later, Donald appeared at my door saying "*you have not been near the boat for weeks*", I agreed, he realised that the experience had affected me and that I was more or less "afraid" to go on the boat again.

Donald spent some time convincing me that I **had** to get back on the boat soon or I never would.

We made our way down to the boat club and reluctantly I got on board with Donald and after a couple of hours on the water my confidence returned.

I owe Donald very sincere thanks for his assistance or I may never have sailed again

A Bigger and Better Boat

In 1990 there was a centenary regatta to celebrate 100 years of the Forth Bridge, most of the club members sailed down from Blackness to take part in this historic event.

This was the last big event I would attend with "*Sonsie,*" as Dan Markey, true to his word phoned me to tell me he was buying a bigger boat and was giving me first refusal on *"Fat Sam".* I asked for time to arrange finance, this he agreed to and before the end of that season I was the proud owner of "*Fat Sam*".

Fat Sam racing on the Forth 1990

I had no trouble at all selling the Silhouette but I was so disappointed that the chap that bought it left it lying on its mooring for a full two seasons and did no maintenance on her at all. It broke my heart to see her falling into disrepair. He finally sold her and she was taken away somewhere else.

As an interesting little aside, Dan Markey has always named his boat with SAM in the name, I don't recall what his "Manta" was called but after "*Fat Sam*" he named his Leisure 23 "*Alaka Sam*", he then had an E Boat which he named "*Play it again*" (after the frequently misquoted line from Casablanca "*play it again, Sam*"). Dan was out of sailing for a few years and blames a conversation with me for him buying another boat, in 2010 a *Saddler 26*, which after his son Daniel asked him "*are you calling it Sam again?*" He has indeed called it: "*Sam Agen*"

At this time other members had also "gone bigger" Donald as I mentioned, had a Vivacity *20 "Play Misty*". Tam Linton also had a *Vivacity 20* called "*Sona*"; Jack Young had an *Alacrity 20* which is very similar to the *Vivacity.* Joe McCrystal now had a *Leisure 23* called "*Eclipse*" and Dan Markey had the *Leisure SL 23 "Alakasam*".

The first race I competed in as the owner of "*Fat Sam*" was a round the islands race which took in the islands of the Firth of Forth, *Inchkeith* being the main one. To give myself a better chance, I asked

Dan Markey to act as crew, as he knew all the little secrets to making her perform better. The longest leg was the beat down to *Inchkeith* and it was here that I learned just how close to the wind this boat could sail. It seemed to defy the rule that bilge keeled boats do not "point" well. This boat seemed to want to point higher and I had to watch that I did not "pinch" but she performed exceptionally well.

By the time we were half way round I could see that we were in a very good position and believed, on handicap, we were by far in the best position. On the run up under the Forth Bridges we flew the spinnaker, something I was not used to, but watching Dan adjust the sheets I soon understood what was what -monkey see monkey do! We pulled further ahead of the others of similar handicaps and when we crossed the line we just *knew* we had won!

With only a couple of weeks left to the end of that season I practically lived on the boat, every free moment I had I was down at the club and felt so disappointed when the day of the "crane out" arrived. The winter of that year seemed the longest I have ever experienced; I could not wait for the "crane in" of the spring.

My performances in the local club races showed a marked improvement and I began winning on a very regular basis. Some of the club members complained that my handicap must be wrong; I of course replied:

"It's the sailor, not the boat!"

One of our neighbouring clubs at Limekilns, on the opposite side of the Firth, annually held a prestigious race called the "Driftwood Trophy".
I had taken part in the past with the Silhouette, but was never a threat to anyone.
I decided to enter with my new secret weapon. On this occasion I chose Donald Thomson as my crew and we set off across the firth like Vikings on a raid.

We were one of the first boats over the line after the starting gun and I was extremely pleased with my perfect start.
With so many different classes of boats in the race, many with handicaps I did not know, it was difficult to work out how well we were doing.
As we turned the penultimate mark, which was quite a short run, Donald suggested we hoist the spinnaker again, I said I did not think it worth the effort for such a short run. Donald replied *"every second counts!"*
I conceded and we raised it for the short leg, dropping it just before turning the last mark for the beat to the finish line.

Following the race, we sat in their clubhouse with beef burgers and lagers awaiting the results. We had won!
The boat we had beaten into second place was only **two seconds** behind us on corrected time:
Donald was right: ***every second counts.***

Me with the "Driftwood Trophy"

With my confidence growing by the day, the honours kept coming; I was regularly in the first three and very often the winner. This was very gratifying, because I was sailing against some very good and competitive sailors.

There were also a lot of excellent sailors in the other clubs in and around the firth. Some of the traveller series we took part in were very well attended and the camaraderie before and after the competitions was first class, however when it came to sailing in races, no quarter was asked and none given.
Sometimes though, circumstances bring you back to earth with a bang!

Pride cometh before a fall.

I recall at one regatta, on the Saturday, after the race, all the competitors were trying to get a berth on the pier next to the clubhouse, all mooring bow in.

There was one space which was nearest the club, knowing I had enough water beneath the keel I made for that position.

The wind was blowing from the west so that I could turn into the wind and stop at the pier. I came in with full sails at a reasonable speed, sailed up to the berth, turned into the wind and stopped about two inches from the pier, stepped ashore with the head rope, looked at the crowd watching me and shouted *"Am I some sailor or what?"*

The following day in similar circumstances I attempted to repeat the performance but with a slight misjudgement, instead of stopping at the pier, I rammed it at about 2 knots, as I stepped ashore with the head rope, the windows of the clubhouse were thrown open and in unison everyone shouted *"are you some sailor or what?"*

At this regatta that some of the visiting yachts, finding that our lads had taken the honours in the first second and third positions, made the remark that we were big fish in a small pond at this end of the firth and we would not do so well in a big regatta such as the Carl Dyson Trophy at Port Edgar.

We accepted this remark as a challenge and the members went down mob handed for that particular regatta a few weeks later.

The Club performed very well. As the small fish in a big pond we took 1st, 2nd, 3rd, 5th and 6th in our class and a had a particularly good write up in Yachting Monthly, stating that Tam Linton, with *"Sona"* and Donald Thomson with *"Play Misty"* who were first and second *"sailed their small cruisers like dinghies"*

Tam Linton in *"Sona"*

Donald Thomson in *"Play Misty"*

55

One of the most endearing things I remember about Blackness, was the terrific banter, if you had no sense of humour you were in the wrong club.

I remember an incident with Dan Markey's wife, Kathryn

I had been away sailing for a few days and on my return to the clubhouse, I decided to have a shower before opening the bar and having myself a drink, a committee privilege at the time. I showered and dried myself off and feeling better I went through to pour myself a large one before dressing, thinking I was still alone in the clubhouse. Dan and Kathryn had come in without my hearing them and as I walked back through into the clubrooms with only a towel round my waist, I saw Kathryn.

In my state of undress I tried to make light of the situation by saying *"don't you think I have the body of Adonis?"* to which Kathryn replied *"you better give it back to him, you've wrinkled it!"*

A young man who worked for me at Unichem, Derek McKain wanted to know more about sailing and asked if he could join me on the boat one day, I of course agreed. On the day, he turned up he brought his uncle, Jim McKain along, who was to become a very good friend of mine.

They both joined me for a sail that day and Jim later became a member and bought his first boat, a *Leisure 17.*

We had at that time an annual cruise called the "Commodore's Cruise" and as I was the commodore at the time I organised it. Jim being very inexperienced in sailing boats asked us to keep an eye on him. There were about a dozen crews taking part in the cruise, many of them who had never sailed into Cramond, a very tricky entrance where you had to follow a haphazard line of poles in sunk into the mud, following the course of the river. I had agreed earlier at the briefing that I would drop anchor off Cramond Island and wait until the last boat caught up with us before leading them all in. I was at anchor with several others waiting for the stragglers, Jim being one of them. When we looked back up the Forth under the bridges, we were convinced that Jim had gone into Port Edgar, so the rest of us lifted our anchors and headed in. I was leading the whole fleet and had a loudspeaker out on the foredeck belting out Wagner's "*Ride of the Bakeries*". The moorings in Cramond are on trots on the river, with high-sided cliffs either side. The sight and sound of us coming in must have been impressive!

Later on when in the clubhouse, Jim McKain who had not in fact gone into Port Edgar and was worried that he might run aground coming into Cramond when trying to navigate his way into the river mouth, stormed up to me and grabbed me by the lapels. "*Y*ou b******! *You ran off and left me!*"

I tried to explain and assured him that by the time he arrived the tide was very high and he was in no danger of running aground. *"I wasn't to know that"* he said. Of course, he was right; I should have checked on him and not left him to his own devices.

I don't think he ever forgave me for that and I have never left anyone since.

Another incident concerning Cramond was when I took John Dixon sailing, I had taken him out once before and he loved it, he now asked me if I would take him and his son out. His son was a very quiet lad under normal circumstances but had "behaviour problems" and John thought that a trip on the boat would calm him down. As it turned out this was indeed the case and the boy seemed to take to me immediately and hung on every word I said, he asked loads of pertinent questions and showed a really keen interest in everything I did or said. We had decided to take a trip to Cramond and as I was negotiating the tricky course into the course of the river he watched me with eagle eyes, as we approached the final hazard (the cill on the river bed) I shouted *"ok fenders over the side. "*
Eager to please me the boy grabbed my biggest most expensive fender and threw it over the side.
I yelled *"I meant tie it on first!"* I watched, helplessly as the tide swept the fender from out of our reach.
Lesson learned: ***Make yourself clear and understood!***

The "Special" Race

There is another story that my old friend, Donald Thomson, manages to raise at every opportunity, much to my embarrassment.

At one of the "Carl Dyson" Regattas at Port Edgar we ventured down as a club, all the boat owners/skippers at Blackness had assembled at the clubhouse before sailing down to Queensferry for the start of the race. Jim McKain was my crew for the day.

We had a quick pint in the clubhouse before we set off and the barmaid Mavis said that she had been instructed by the bar convener to get rid of some "out of date" bottles of *Carlsberg Special Brew*. She explained that she was to sell them off at 50p a bottle.

Never one to miss a bargain, I bought the last dozen bottles. Hanging around to get the bottles into the boat made me a little late in leaving and I was a fair bit behind the others as they made their way to the start off Port Edgar Marina, we had entered by post earlier in the week.

As I approached the start line I was at the wrong end of the line for the wind that was blowing. All the other boats (around 50-60) were at the other end on the line waiting for the start gun. As the gun went off the whole fleet was becalmed, except for one little boat, which was at the wrong end! I found myself sailing well and in the right direction when every other boat was completely static.

Those at the opposite end of the line remained in a pocket of "still airs" for the best part of an hour.

"Fat Sam" had made such good time; all we had to do was finish the race and we would have won. In hindsight, my decision, at this point to open our cheap beer and have a celebratory drink was without doubt, a grave mistake!

I became so imbibed, I made a load of poor decisions and ended up in the tidal eddy at Hound Point and was making no headway as the rest of the fleet sailed past, in the now fair wind. When "Fat Sam" finally motored into the marina, Jim was at the helm and according to witnesses; I fell out of the boat onto the pontoon.

A lot more Cruising

Now owning a boat that had full standing headroom, I did a lot more cruising than I had in the past. I remember taking Steve and one of his mates Shug Ilgunas on a weeklong trip. We just started by playing it by ear and worked the passages on a daily basis. The first stop was Aberdour, which was an easy hop from Blackness. We had a few beers at night and set off in the morning heading for Anstruther. We had a fried breakfast of bacon, eggs, beans and toast before leaving and after washing up the dishes we set sail.

The wind was "fresh" but not too bad and the sea as far as I was concerned was slight. Shug soon became very sea sick and brought up his breakfast over the stern.

"I won't give you a breakfast again if you going to feed it to the fish!" I said. I thought his **Mal de mer** would wear off, but he only got worse and by the time we were level with Elie, we sailed into that fine little harbour.

We advised Shug to go and find a chemist and buy some Stugeron®, Steve and I waited on the boat for him coming back and after an hour we began to get worried so went off in search of him. Shug is a great rock climber and we found him climbing up a rough brick wall around 20ft high, he seemed quite happy so we left him and went to the pub.

A while later we saw Shug walk past the pub in the direction of the town and wondered where he had gone, around 30 minutes later he appeared in the pub but did not feel like a drink. We discussed our options as it was now pouring with rain and we opted for staying the night here in Elie.

Shug then disappeared again, so Steve and I had another pint. By the time Shug returned yet again the rain had become a thunderstorm with lightning flashing across the sky. Steve asked, "*What would happen if we were still out there?*" I replied "W*e would not have to charge the batteries for several years!*"

Shug made several trips up to the town and each time he came back with something new, a comb, a toothbrush and some batteries. It turned out that he had taken a shine to the girl serving in the chemist shop.

"*Why don't you just ask for condoms and be done with it?*" I asked?

Shug found this decidedly unfunny.

The following morning, we decided to head for Dunbar and I set a course for the Bass Rock, which would be just less than 10 miles away. Not long after we left the harbour, a thick fog came down and with Steve on the helm I told him that he <u>must</u> steer the compass course I had given him. I stayed below most of the time, working on the charts to plot our estimated position every 15 to 20 min, as this was long before we had the luxury of GPS, asking Steve the distance we had covered on the log.

At one point, whilst I was in the cockpit, we heard the throb of large diesel engines, but we were unable to determine from which direction the sound was coming. Suddenly this coaster loomed though the fog, no more than 100 feet from us and on a collision course: I quickly turned the tiller to port to escape certain death and the coaster slid past us. There was no sign of anyone on watch and here were no fog signals at all.

As soon as it had passed, the wake threw us all over the place; we had just had the narrowest of escapes. We sat in silence for a minute or two when Shug said, *"I wish we were on the Titanic!"*
I asked *"Why?"*
He replied, *"Well at least they had a band!"*

Our next problem was not far away, I had plotted our course using estimated positioning, allowing for what effect the tide was having on us and what little leeway we were experiencing so to my reckoning, we should have soon been able see the Bass Rock, God knows it's big enough.

With all eyes and ears on alert, Shug thought he could hear waves breaking, sure enough in a short time we could see the waves breaking on a rocky outcrop, but this was not the Bass Rock.
The fog lifted enough for me to see that although it had a light; it was nowhere near big enough to be what we were looking for. I quickly went below

again studied the chart and realised we were at Fidra. Five bloody miles west of where we should have been.

Steve, not believing in the course I had given him, was sailing on what he *thought* was the correct course, this is a common phenomenon in fog with inexperienced sailors, so I could not berate him, I only hoped that he had learned his lesson.

This change in our circumstances made me change my mind as to our planned destination and we set a new course for Newhaven, where we arrived safely. We had a few beers in the Newhaven Boat Club that night before sailing home to Blackness the following morning.

Jim goes Bigger

Jim McKain had not kept the Leisure 17 for long and soon had a larger *Leisure* in the 22-foot version; this was called **"Puffin"**. Jim and I went on many short cruises together; some sailors even remarked that as we were seen together on the water so often, that I should change the name of my boat to Blawin' (Blowing) we could then be referred to as
"Puffin and Blawin"

Jim McKain with *"Puffin"*

One night after sailing down to Elie, again, we were in the local pub when a man seeing us in sailing gear started asking questions about our boats, we thought he was speaking quite knowledgably about them, *"what kind of boat is yours?"* he asked Jim *"Leisure 22"* replied Jim *"and you?"* he asked me, I said *"A Sunray 21"* he then continued with what we both thought were relevant sailing questions until Jim asked him what kind of boat he had, he answered *"A blue one"* Jim and I fell about laughing and he left quite quickly.

Misplaced Humour & Lost Weekends

My marriage had been on a rocky foundation for some time and I did not help the situation by being off on the boat as much as I was.

One remark that I made, trying to be funny, certainly was not taken as the humour it was meant to be.

I wanted to get an even bigger boat and having seen a Westerly Centaur on the market for a very good price, I said to Ellen that I was thinking of buying it.

"Over my dead body!" She said.

I replied, *"The price was attractive enough, but that sounds even better!"*

During this period, I must admit that I was completely selfish with my sailing, my job could be quite stressful, this coupled with my problems at home made me just want to escape. I would often leave my work on the Friday afternoon, go right down to the boat and sail off into the sunset, not returning until the weekend had finished, have a shower and go straight back out to work again.

I remember one evening this behaviour came to a head at home and Ellen confronted me with it. She said *"last weekend you just disappeared on the boat, you didn't even phone, for all I knew you could have been in Davy Jones' Locker. "*
My son Stuart, who was witnessing the discussions, said *"more likely he would have been in Davy Jones' pub!"*
I was being unfair but it is a bit late to repent now.

On one of my "lost" weekends I had sailed right down as far as the Farne Islands and when returning I heard the forecast for *"Easterlies force 6 gusting 7"* I figured I could handle this and kept sailing homeward. As I was sailing past Eyemouth, the next forecast issued a gale warning in sea area Forth & Tyne and was imminent.
The winds being easterly were "onshore" and trying to find shelter on the coast was completely out of the question!

For once they got the forecast right and I was reefed down as far as I could and spent the next thirteen hours hanging onto the tiller for dear life. I could not let go of the helm at all and when I wanted to have a basic bodily function I did where I was, fully clothed.

That is probably the most frightening experience of my life; you will <u>know</u> if you ever reach that point, when looking at huge waves and you start talking to the boat, I kept saying, "*We'll never get over this one*"

It was bad enough when the boat was on a reach but when I turned into the Firth of Forth after St Abb's Head; the waves seemed even bigger when behind me.   That experience taught me a very valuable lesson: it's not the boat that will fail in those conditions; it is more than likely the man will fail first. I now had the utmost confidence in my boat.

My "lost" weekends continued and not surprisingly in 1992 my wife Ellen and I separated. I carried on with my job for a while after this but as I had never really been happy in Livingston, apart from the sailing, I wanted a move.
I visited my mother in Cromarty, when she was staying with a very good friend of hers and was invited to stay over for Christmas 1992.
I got on so well with Lilly, my mum's friend who was same age as me that I came back for the New Year. I then started to come up every two weeks then every week until I decided to cut all ties down south and move to Cromarty.

I carried on sailing when I could at Blackness while making arrangements to start my own business in the Highlands. Lilly would join me a couple of times at Blackness for weekends on the boat during the start of summer 1993.

Lilly on "Fat Sam" on the Forth

I had hoped to start trading by April but circumstances conspired against me, it was August before that happened. In June I decided to sail *"Fat Sam"* up the coast to my new home in Cromarty.

Before I left the Club members arranged a big farewell party for me and gave me an album with photographs of all the different parties, cruises, races and other events I had shared with them over the years I was at Blackness. Everyone signed the inside of it with personal messages wishing me good luck. It was a very nice touch; I do miss them all very much. A few weeks later I sailed down the Forth for the last time.

Tam Linton agreed to crew me all the way to Cromarty and for that I was grateful. We had planned to leave on the Saturday morning but suddenly realised there was a big race on the Saturday with a prize of £50 to the winner. That was too good an opportunity to miss and Tam agreed we should stay and compete. We had a fairly good start and were in a fair position, but as the race went on Donald Thomson and another boat that I can't remember were leaving me behind.

As the two boats ahead of me rounded the last mark before the finish it was obvious by their course heading that they were making for another mark of the course instead of the finish line. When I turned the mark, I had to make it look as if I too was heading for the mark until I was sure I could beat them to the line. This I managed to do and when I altered course to the finish line, they saw me but as they told me later they thought I had made a mistake.

I crossed the line and received the finishing sound signal, I had won and the money was in the bag. First rule of yacht racing
"Read the sailing instructions".

Heading for Pastures New

After we picked up the prize money we said our last goodbyes and set sail for Cromarty. The first night we only got as far as Crail on the Fife coast. On Sunday we sailed with the tide and rounded Fife Ness and with a good following wind from the South West we made excellent time covering fifty nautical miles before deciding to put into a fine little harbour at Gourdon.

There is an excellent little fresh fish shop where we bought our supper and cooked it on board before we retired to a pub right on the harbour, what more could one ask for?

At first light next morning we set sail and by mid afternoon we had completed a further 45 miles and were just off Peterhead, there was a thick fog descending and we decided to put into Peterhead to wait for it to clear. We were stuck in this port for three days as the weather had taken a turn for the worst with the fog lasting two full days followed strong wind warnings.

By Thursday morning the wind had eased a little and we set off again in a force 4 from the east and had an interesting sail round Rattray Head, I was at the Helm and Tam was below doing the chart work.

"Fat Sam" in Peterhead Harbour

As we approached Rattray Head, a trawler had which had overtaken us about ten minutes earlier, was now about half a mile ahead and he seemed to disappear in huge troughs of water caused by the meeting of the tides. I called to Tam to quickly close the weatherboards and for about twenty minutes we experienced *"Fat Sam"* burying her nose in the huge waves caused by the tide race, the water at times coming up over the coach roof to the height of the gooseneck on the boom. We gave a sigh of relief when we eventually cleared it and set a course for Cromarty along the Moray coast; at last we were getting somewhere again.

However our happiness and contentment was short lived as the fog rolled in again forcing us to put into Fraserburgh. By this time we had swapped positions, with Tam was now on the helm and me navigating. This was long before I could afford the luxury of GPS, which by then was being made available to the leisure sailors of the world at an astronomically high price.

I plotted a course for Fraserburgh harbour using dead reckoning and allowing for leeway and tidal drift I gave Tam the course to steer, Tam steering in limited visibility needed to have full confidence in the course I supplied and not repeat the same error as Steven, my son had when sailing towards Bass Rock.

After a while Tam said, quite casually "*I think you need to look at this.* "
I stuck my head out of the hatchway, and looked ahead only to see water crashing over rocks, I yelled "*Come about for Gods sake*!"
Tam asked "*What course*"?
"*The reciprocal of what we were on. We hit nothing on the way in!*"
I exclaimed

What we had been seeing was Colonel Rock 1M ENE of Fraserburgh, my calculation for leeway and the tide had been a little out. In this situation with nothing to see from which to take a bearing, I estimated our position, plotted a new course and we sailed into Fraserburgh Bay, still sailing blind. I decided to put on the depth sounder to try and follow the contour line of the bottom round the bay into the harbour. Tam wanted to leave the sounder on all the time, but with an independent battery it used power very quickly and would not have lasted long at all.

I switched it on, checked the depth then turned it off again. Tam immediately turned it on again.

What happened next seems so funny on hindsight, but at the time it shocked us both back into total concentration.   We saw above us, through the gloom, a row of caravans.   This meant we were much closer to the shore than we should be, in fact, right under the caravan site.

With the panic earlier, I had not made my calculations to allow for the tide height and we were using the wrong contour line. At least we now knew where we were, albeit too close to the shore, we steered into deeper water and hoped we were heading in the right direction and with a certain amount of relief, we spotted the lighthouse on the end of the breakwater. By the time we entered the harbour, the visibility was down to twenty yards.

The Harbour Master was surprised to see us when we appeared from nowhere, asking, "W*here did you come from*"?

"*Peterhead"* I replied.

"*In this weather?"* he asked.

To which I replied "*It was a dawdle*!"

There is nothing like a bit of bravado to give you a lift when your confidence has been dented.

The fog stayed with us for a further two days and we were fast running out of time to get the boat to Cromarty, I had to get the business up and running and Tam was due back at work soon.

I telephoned my son Steve in Edinburgh, asking him to go to Blackness with my car and pick up the boat trailer and bring it to Fraserburgh.
As we sat in the pub later, fortune smiled upon us for once. We started got talking to some lads who had their own mobile crane, which they operated within the harbour and agreed to lift "*Fat Sam*" onto the trailer for a very good price.

When Steve arrived that night the boat was lifted on and tied down and all three of had to climb up to get into our bunks for the night. The next day, we spent driving to Cromarty, much to the relief of Lilly who had been worrying about us.

The final incident of the trip occurred as we drove past Forres. Steve was at the wheel when he noticed what he described as a "bumping feeling" through the steering as we negotiated a roundabout, I asked him to pull in at the next convenient spot and a check round the trailer then the car, I noticed that one of the allow wheels on the car had been working loose. I jacked it up and tightened that wheel and checked all the others. Thankfully no damage had been done to the wheel and the remainder of the journey to Cromarty was uneventful.

Tam and Steve both stayed with us a Cromarty for a night and in the morning I ran them both into Inverness to catch the train back to Edinburgh.

Within a few days of arriving in Cromarty I had arranged for a berth in the harbour and launched the boat and she took up residence in her new home.

"Fat Sam" moored in her new home at Cromarty

A Fresh Start

When I first arrived in Cromarty with "Fat Sam", I wanted to join a boat club and the nearest to me was Chanonry Sailing Club at Fortrose. I applied to join and was accepted. The first few times I was at the club I tried to make friends with some of the other sailors, which I found very difficult.

Normally sailing is a great leveller and no matter what anyone does for a living the love of sailing usually gives the necessary bond. I found Fortrose unique on this point, nobody there wanted to talk to me at all. They all seemed to, look down their noses at me and would ignore me when I spoke to them. Perhaps I just happened to bump into the wrong folk when I went round.

The Club in fact did and still does, a wonderful job in training youngsters in a very healthy dinghy section, but the cruiser at that time, 1993-94, seemed to be very pretentious, thinking they were better than most.

However,there was one sailor there that I had come in contact with on the water but never really had a conversation with him, as I only saw when competing in the 1994 Moray Firth Cruiser race. His name was Tim McKeggie and his boat was a *Hurley 24/70* named *"Norseman"*. We were racing against each other; his handicap was unknown to me. We seemed to be neck and neck all the way and at the end of the race I awaited the results and was somewhat disappointed to find out he had won and I think I was 4th that year. I had no idea what other boats had beaten me.

I only stayed at Fortrose Club for one season, opting to try the next nearest club, which was Invergordon Boating Club. Here I found a great bunch of lads and enjoyed their company very much indeed.

They had a terrific sailing programme, packed with regular races but unfortunately for me they were all geared towards those boats a lot bigger and a lot faster than my 21ft Sunray.

Their fleet consisted of Hunter Impalas and Sonatas and several other very fast racing boats, for me to try and compete against these was impossible.

Invergordon Boating Club are the organisers of the Moray Firth Cruiser Race, which I entered again in 1995, only to beaten yet again by *"Norseman"* who was first again, I had faired a little better than the previous year coming in third, the boat coming second was a *Balaton 24*.

I stayed at the Invergordon Club for two seasons but soon realised that to get racing with boats my own size and speed I would have to start a boat club of my own in Cromarty.

With the help of Alex Davidson, I formed the Cromarty Boat Club and we were instrumental in getting the boat compound and later the Tower renovated for the use of the Club

The start of Cromarty Boat Club

Toward the end on **1995** I wrote a letter to the local papers asking for anyone interested in forming a boat club at Cromarty to come to a public meeting to discuss the possibilities.

The response was overwhelming with over fifty people turning up to the meeting. I acted as Chairman for the meeting and answered all their questions with candour and advised that the best way forward would be to elect a steering committee from those assembled to make up the bones of a club with a constitution and rules etc.

The assembled crowd agreed then immediately started to nominate each other to sit onto the steering committee.

As I was relatively unknown to most of them, my name was not put forward. I called for order and pointed out that as the only one present that had substantial experience in the running of a boat club it might be prudent to nominate me! I was voted in as chairman of the steering committee.

Under my guidance, the steering committee drew up a constitution and a set of rules, the number of office bearers and committee required and the aims of the club. We then called a second meeting to elect the Executive Officers and committee of the "Cromarty Boat Club" and in March of 1996, my ambition and dream had been fulfilled.

New ties and old friends

Lilly and I had been getting closer and closer and we realised we were meant for each other and we married on the 27th April **1996**, we invited a lot of my friends from Blackness to the wedding, it was great to have them all round me again.

After I launched the boat in 1996, I had been teaching my stepson Kevin how to sail and every time I took him out, the conditions were ideal for sailing. He, like me many years before was fascinated in how a boat can sail to windward and with speed and elegance. He wanted it to go even faster and kept asking for more wind. I said "*you don't want any more wind Kev' this is ideal*".

The Moray Firth Cruiser Race came round yet again and I entered with Kev' as my crew. The race traditionally starts at Findhorn and races back to Cromarty. There were three classes with varying courses so that theoretically, they should cross the line in a pretty close finish. To allow our boats to get to the start line we would normally have had to leave Cromarty in the early hours, dependent on the wind, to travel the fifteen miles to the start.

In the race of June 1996, the wind was from the west and was fairly brisk so we did not have to leave until 0830 and we had a great run over for the 1200 start.

We arrived in plenty time and had to sail about for almost an hour before the start. The wind had been rising steadily since we left and was around a force 7 at the start. This rose even further within an hour of the start. We were now racing, fully reefed down in a force 8 on a beat, sailing to windward. The movement in the boat was quite bad and Kevin, who had been on the drink the night before, was starting to feel really bad and was throwing up over the stern with alarming regularity. I had also been drinking the night before and although I did not feel great, I was not sick like Kevin. He looked absolutely awful, I said, *"You've got wind Kev, do you like it?"* Again *"Norseman"* beat me, but at least now I was second.

Peter Robertson in his new boat *"Shadowfax"*, a *Sadler 26* with Tam Linton and Jim McKain as crew, sailed up from Blackness and they arrived on the Saturday afternoon having sailed non stop from the Firth of Forth. They had a couple of days rest at Cromarty then Tam made his way home by bus and Peter and Jim continued on a cruise to the west coast via the Caledonian Canal. I decided to take a few days off work with Lilly and accompany them some of the way through the canal with *"Fat Sam"*.

The weather could not have been kinder to us; with glorious sunshine for the time we were away with them. This had been my first experience of the canal and the same for Lilly. We sailed with them, as far as the Great Glen Water Park when we had to turn back home and wished them fair winds for the rest of their cruise. Lilly and I returned to Cromarty to get back to work.

"Shadowfax" and *"Fat Sam"* at Muirton Locks

Two days after we arrived home I got a call from Peter, asking if he could leave his boat at Cromarty, as he had been informed that his wife Liz had been diagnosed with a serious ilness and he was now on his way back up the canal.

I asked him where he was calling from and he replied "*Laggan Locks*". I figured I could drive down to meet him at Fort Augustus, give him my van and I could bring his boat back to Cromarty with Jim thus letting him get down the road to see Liz.

This is exactly what we did and sailing *"Shadowfax"* back to Cromarty was an added bonus to me. It was the first time I had the chance to use a GPS and I was mightily impressed.

As our first Regatta was on the last weekend of July and after enquiring about Liz I asked Peter, if I could use his boat to race in our regatta to which he agreed. *"Shadowfax"* had all the gizmos for telling the skipper wind speed, direction, rudder position and any other information you needed to sail a boat. Jim was watching all the instruments and kept shouting, *"That's it! You have it perfect!"* not realising I was ignoring all the fancy gear and sailing "by the seat of my pants". We did very well that day, gaining a third place against all the big Invergordon boats.

Alex Davidson was controlling the race from a tent on the links and Moray Firth Radio were giving "live" coverage of our first regatta and wanted to speak to me via VHF, I ended up giving a rendition of "Sweet Caroline" over the radio, and yes, I do know it is illegal.

Peter's wife Liz did improve and made a full recovery.

In June of **1997**, I entered the Moray Firth Cruiser Race yet again, with Alex Davidson as my crew and the wind was blowing very hard from the east. We raced up and down the start line, waiting for the off, I said that we would keep the reefs in the sails until the gun and then shake them out for the obvious "run" home.

As soon as the race started, I shook out the reefs and the boat took off. A few of the bigger boats were trying to fly their spinnakers and Alex asked, *"Are we going put up our spinnaker?"* I replied *"we're doing twice the optimum speed now; I don't think the boat would stand it!"* The log on *"Fat Sam"* only went to 10 knots and the needle was already hitting that on occasions, the whole boat was vibrating when it did, we must have been putting a lot of strain on the rigging and the spars.

The race had started at 1200 and at 1400 we were sailing through the Sutors having sailed over 15 nautical miles. We had won!

Lilly and I with the winners cup

Expanding the Club

Cromarty 2000, a company set up locally, was already proposing radical changes to the harbour and the surrounding area and expressed a delight at the forming of a boat club, which they believed, would strengthen their case. It is extremely unfortunate that their project failed at the last hurdle and was unsuccessful in obtaining the necessary funding.

They say that every cloud has a silver lining and this turned out to be ours. The old lookout tower had featured prominently in the refurbishment plans of the harbour area, now with the collapse of the project this was left without interest from any other party.

I then contacted Michael Nightingale, the owner, to discuss the possibility of taking a lease on the tower. Letters went back and forward but progress was very slow due to the ill health of Michael Nightingale.
The boat club was going from strength to strength; the regatta was fast becoming one of the "places to be" events on the sailing calendar.

The **1998** season started well, with some weekend sailing to places a little further a field and more sailors actually joining the club. We were starting to look quite professional, with several moorings in the bay, whereas in 1996, I had been the sole yacht out there, we now had around ten moorings and more sailors were making enquiries for membership.

The British Legion Club in Cromarty was an obvious attraction for visiting yachts, but it too was starting to wane. The Moray Firth Cruiser Race, which used to attract over fifty yachts, had started to dwindle slightly too but still attracted numbers around 30.

I competed again in the Moray Firth Cruiser Race but could not repeat my win of the previous year.

Alex's Hangover

In June my old mate, Joe McCrystal had bought a Mirage 28 which was lying in Nairn harbour and he and his wife, Annette, along with Donald Thomson and another Blackness member came up to sail it back down the coast. I agreed to sail over with Alex to Nairn and have a few beers with them and see them off in the morning. On our way I said to Alex, *"Don't try to keep up with these guys drinking. They're professionals"* needless to say he did not take my advice, and on our return journey back to Cromarty, Alex was decidedly unwell.

Moving Forward

The Commodore's Cruise, which I had introduced just after the club was formed, now made an attempt at reaching Orkney. After an overnight stop in Lybster, we sailed up to Wick, but unfortunately the weather deteriorated and we would spend the next three days waiting for a window in the weather to make the run for home.

The regatta continued to be popular and onshore events were a big attraction for many visitors from the surrounding area.

Unfortunately, Michael Nightingale died in September before we reached an agreement on the tower.
The whole idea was shelved after this; however Alex and I continued to discuss all the possibilities. One plan included approaching Michael's son, John, to try to negotiate leasing the land around the harbour, which until now had been nothing but an eyesore, and of course to try and re-open negotiations on the tower.

We presented our case to the committee, who readily agreed and Alex and myself were given a mandate to obtain leases on both projects. Right from the very start, John Nightingale was extremely helpful and we started to make headway on our plans.

There was such a lot going on at the boat club that the cruising side took a little dip and we had only a small cruise in **1999** for around four or five boats, down the canal to Banavie, to the top of Neptune's Staircase, and back. The break was fine for us, but it was probably the most uneventful cruise, so much so, that I kept no record of it and nothing of any significance happened to make it unforgettable.

In **2000**, another attempt would be made to reach Orkney. I had my youngest son, Stuart, with me. He had never really been interested in sailing but felt that he would like to join me for this trip, perhaps he wanted a bit of bonding, but as he was then 33 years old it might have been a little late. He proved to be good company and he had asked if his mate, Mark Macbeth could join us.

Bill Paterson had no crew so we arranged for the Mark to join us at Wick on the Monday; he would arrive there by bus.

Two other boats were with us, Rod MacIntosh with his wife, Sandra, in their *Westerly 25 "Katra"* and a friend of his, from Avoch with a home made, home designed, steel boat, who tended to keep himself to himself.

On the Saturday, we sailed as far as Helmsdale, which at 30 miles, was far enough for Bill being single-handed and then on to Wick the following morning.

We were about two hours into the trip to Wick, when the wind started to rise quite quickly. I said to Stuart *"I need to put a reef in the main"* with Stuart having no idea what I was talking about, I explained as simply as I could, that all he had to do was steer the boat and I would go up to the mast to take in the reef. I handed over the tiller and stepped up onto the coach roof with reefing handle in my hand.

"Fat Sam" has a roller reefing boom, not the best, but then who cares about the "sail shape" when the wind gets up?
I was standing with my back to the foresail and winding the boom round whilst letting out the main halyard with my other hand. Stuart was sailing the boat on the foresail alone.
I say he was sailing the boat, although that might be a slight exaggeration.

He allowed the jib to backfill and the boat spun round to port; the foresail with a very strong wind against it now had me pinned against the mast. The boat was now sailing Stuart!
He sat there with the tiller pointing skywards yelling, *"We are going to die! You said this wasn't dangerous!"*

I was trying to get him to release the jib sheet from the cleat to let me get away from this position and get control of the boat again.

After a few choice expletives delivered at the top of my voice he at last complied with my request and we got everything sorted out.
Rounding Clythe Ness is always uncomfortable with the tidal effect on the water; this also made Stuart a

little uncomfortable.   The remainder of the trip to Wick was a little quiet, not the wind, but Stuart.

On the Monday morning, as I made my back from the shower block, I was climbing down the ladder to the boat.   The ladders are set into the harbour wall and when the tide is out it is about fifteen feet from the top down to the boat and with seaweed growth on the rungs they can be quite dodgy.

I was about half way down when I lost my footing and with the toilet gear in one hand only had one hand to hold on, I was unable to keep my grip and fell awkwardly onto the boat.   My legs were over the side but my torso landed on the top of the guardrail giving my ribs a crack.

I was in considerable pain when we walked up to town to meet the Inverness bus with Bill's new crewmember aboard.

On our return to the boat Mark was last to come down the ladder and he too slipped and landed in the water.

Instinct made me grab out for him and as I tried to pull him back onto the boat, I exacerbated my already tender rib cage.

A short while afterwards we sailed out toward Duncansby Head, but feeling the way I did, I felt it would be unwise to attempt crossing the Pentland Firth.   I radioed Bill to tell him that I was turning back and he did the same.   Rod went on to have a really good week exploring Scapa Flow with his friend.

We opted to have an overnight stop at Lybster when heading home and another in Portmahomack, so the trip was not altogether wasted. Mark turned out to be really good company with a sharp wit, he had this catch phrase that he seemed use all the time when we were in a discussion about anything, he would suddenly say *"are we sure this cant be resolved with violence?"* We had all enjoyed the trip but I was disappointed that Orkney had eluded me yet again.

By the start of **2001**, we had lease agreements on both the boat park project and the tower. The leases both came into effect on the 1st of January. The boat park was for a period of ten years and the tower, for a period of twenty-five years.

We had heard through the grapevine that the Community Council was possibly going to lodge an objection with the planning department, regarding our plans for the compound. I made a presentation at a Community Council meeting, after which they agreed to support us.

The problem now was where to get the money. Realising we could only tackle one problem at a time; we opted for the easier of the two to start.

Although red tape is notoriously difficult to cut through, we soon had planning permission for the boat park. There were minor hiccups but nothing to really slow us down.

Alex made the raising of the necessary funding look like a cakewalk and he dealt superbly with all the administration even down to organising the contractors we needed.

I dealt with all things technical, directing the contractors to the levelling of the compound and the fencing contractors as to the position and dimensions of posts, gates and materials used, as many items were stipulated within the planning permission.

Both Alex and I feel very proud of the contribution we made to the success of the boat park construction, which was opened and ready for use by the end of the season in 2001.

The New Compound

Alex and I felt that the tower would be a more difficult nut to crack and initially invited professionals to advise us. The firm dealing with the Harbour Trust, as well as the now dormant Cromarty 2000, were asked if they would be interested in acting on our behalf.

After a couple of meetings with the architect, who had very grandiose plans for the structure, I felt that we were being taken down a very long and dark road leading to God knew where?

It is, after all said and done, only a brick building. We needed something useful not a monument.

At the next committee meeting I proposed that we act as our own agents in the project and after a lot of discussion, the committee agreed.

There were times when I felt that we had bitten off more than we could chew, but as time went on we seemed to get better at dealing with problems. Sometimes we had conflict because Alex had said one thing to someone, then I had said something else. We needed to get things straight.

A number of things then happened which had a great impact on the whole project. The opening of the boat park had started to swell our membership and we had attracted some very useful new blood into the club.

To my surprise some of the existing members, such as Charlie Bateman, revealed their knowledge of building and planning, drawing and general construction information, skills of which we made excellent use.

We drew up lists of the necessary tasks, courtesy of Gavin Meldrum, and allotted these tasks to the person most able to do them.

Alex was instructed to get the money at all costs but stay away from contractors. I was told not to have anything to do with the funding people as I might upset them. I cannot imagine how I could ever upset anyone?

Renovating the Tower : L-R Alex Davidson, Ron King
Bill Paterson, Alastair Stewart and Me

On the cruising side, we had made another attempt for Orkney in 2001, on this occasion the weather was against us and we spent three days riding out a storm, again in Wick harbour. It is not an ideal place to spend a holiday, no offence to the "Wickers".

Having only a week to complete the round trip we reluctantly returned to Cromarty, failing miserably once again, much to the delight of the local buffoons in Cromarty, who made derogatory remarks and comments throughout the coming year.

Apart from a couple of weekends in **2002**, this was another season of little or no cruising. I competed again in the Moray Firth Cruiser Race and at the end, although I had crossed the line well ahead of any other in my class, was beaten into second place by the Balaton 24. I tried to protest against his handicap as I thought it was a "bandit" but the organisers, Invergordon Boating Club, dismissed it with Duncan Murray saying, *"It might be something to do with the sailor"*. Again, a case of **"It's the sailor, not the boat."**

The following regatta was Invergordon's own. A number of our club boats went up for the race but again the courses were set for Sonatas and we had not even finished the first race, when the horn sounded to start the second race.

In disgust, I radioed to say I was going back to Cromarty, as the races were not taking the slower classes into account. The other club boats followed me home, which meant there were no slow handicap boats for the Sunday racing. That is apart from one: the Balaton 24.

We later heard that on the Sunday, the Balaton was allowed to compete and they made it one class. The Balaton finished around an hour after anyone else and won the event on handicap.

Allegedly, Duncan Murray was the first to complain that the handicap of the Balaton was wrong. I heard later that the rig on the boat was possibly not the original and was above the spec' for the boat and it could have been sailing with an unfair advantage for years.

Our regatta went ahead as normal, but other cruises and races were somewhat curtailed as we were all preoccupied, most of the committee were involved with projects concerning the ongoing improvements to our club. I did spend a fair bit of time on *"Fat Sam"* teaching a young French couple, Jean Yves Lemmel and Claire Cadet to sail and this helped take my mind off the headaches of the ongoing work.

However all our efforts started to pay dividends and by the end of the season we were in a very favourable position on all fronts.

The start of **2003** was starting to look very promising, contracts were sent out to tender and wherever possible, we asked local tradesmen to quote for all the work. By the end of January most of the applications for funding had gone off to the relevant agencies and the membership sat waiting in anticipation for the word, would we get the money or not?

The Scottish Lottery, Scottish Heritage, Historic Scotland and Awards for All turned us down, as well as a few other organisations. What was more disappointing was being told that we didn't qualify for CED funding, this came from HIE, down through RACE, because we didn't prove any financial benefits for the community. Alex then did some research, wrote a business plan and a brilliant presentation showing that our toilet, showers and washer/dryer were going to bring at least £16,000 a year into Cromarty. Since then, other groups in Ross and Cromarty, requesting funding from CED, have used that same presentation model.

After several frustrating failures, Alex finally came to me with the news that it was all systems "GO".
Work started during the month of March and to start with seemed to take forever to get off the ground; we continually hit little niggling problems that would set us back by several days. We had already decided upon an opening day, which was to be the 5th of May. As the day approached, I was becoming

increasingly more irritable at the set backs and fell out with a couple of the contractors. I also had a set to with Ron King, who had done the structural calculations, insisting on an added leg to put in support, where one of the outriggers had been removed to accommodate the stairway.

He was right of course, but I thought he was being too pedantic and by this time my blood pressure was through the roof.

Gavin, on seeing the state I was getting myself into, made me take a step back from the project for a couple of days.

Notices went out to the membership, asking for any kind of assistance or donations of equipment and it is very gratifying that ninety percent of the membership did work or donated items for the running of the new "Clubhouse". In many cases we had members who donated items and worked on the decorating and landscaping. I think that the project brought us all together so that we gelled into a club at last.

The thanks to everyone were made on the opening day and in the newsletter that followed, however I must say to everyone who contributed, you will never know just how much I appreciated all of your efforts.

The New Clubhouse opened 2003

We now have a very functional clubhouse with tremendous facilities for the visiting yachtsmen who will now start to arrive from all over Europe.

We also have a regular entry in Reeds Almanac, which will ensure our name goes everywhere there are keen sailors.

I wanted to inject some enthusiasm back into the cruising and there had been a boat skippers/owners meeting in January to discuss another attempt at Orkney following those, which had ended in failure.

At the meeting nine boat owners agreed it was

Orkney or Bust!

It was a bit disappointing to find that due to other commitments, a number of boats had to cancel the trip and in the end only three boats went all the way to Orkney.

I was determined I was going at any cost!

The following is an account of that trip.

Saturday 7th June 2003

As I walked the dog just after first light, I could see a lone yacht about a mile beyond the North Sutor.

I assumed this was Bill Paterson and Neil Brooker in "Wigeon" as they had told me the evening before that they intended setting off as soon as dawn had broken. It was, therefore, quite a surprise to see them coming round the point from the harbour as I approached the other end of the links.

I wonder who the other boat is out there.

As "Wigeon" passed the ferry slip, they saw my dog "Corrie" first then me, waving, they shouted, *"We'll see you in Lybster"*

I had wakened Steve before leaving for my walk and hoped that he was up and about by the time I got back. Steve is more like a mate to me than a son but he is not a "morning person" like me and is best left to his own devices until he is fully awake.
Luckily when I opened the door I could immediately see he was at least half-awake and able to conduct a conversation without biting my head off. (When he reads this he will say that it is the other way round)

We took turns in the shower and then had breakfast before heading down to the boat at around 0515.

Jock Wingate in *"Heart of Gold"* who had spent the night alongside in the harbour, was up and about, just finishing his breakfast, Alex Davidson, his crew had already arrived and they were just about ready for the off.
I too had left *"Fat Sam"* in the harbour overnight to make it easier to get aboard with our gear and to cut down the hassle of rowing out to the mooring then

deflating the rubber dinghy. This was already folded and stowed just forward of the mast step.

Gavin Meldrum and his crew Rod Duncan arrived about ten minutes later and were quickly out to their mooring to prepare "*Polar Wind*" for the trip.

Steve and I were ready for sailing by the time the last crew of Peter Baxter and "Pug" Peterson arrived. They took a little while to get organised but were eventually out and aboard "*Norseman*".

Three boats left together, whilst "*Norseman*" took some time to get off her mooring, there was no wind at all at this point and we were all under power. The reflections on the water of both the North and South Sutor looked spectacular. When we live in such close proximity to natural beauty we tend to take it for granted, however, mornings like this have a way of reminding you how lucky you are to be living in such surroundings.

Log reading 4397.5.
Forecast winds light to variable SW. Course to steer from Buss Bank. 030 degrees

I had a little difficulty with the outboard motor on "*Fat Sam*", it was drawing air and we had to stop halfway between the harbour and the Buss Bank to affect a repair.

I cut about an inch from the rubber pipe where it enters the fuel inlet; wear and tear had caused a small fracture, and was under way again within ten minutes. By this time Peter and Pug were just astern of me with the others about half a mile ahead. The time now was 0550.

The tide had only just turned so we would have it in our favour for the next six hours.

The trip from here to Lybster was pretty boring, as we had to motor most of the way. For a period of around an hour a slight breeze did get up from the southwest which allowed me to use my spinnaker, however this was short lived and we were soon back to the Suzuki and its *five horses*.

All the boats had become spread out a bit, but we remained in sight of each other all day arriving at Lybster at about 15-minute intervals with the exception of Bill Paterson who had arrived an hour before any of the rest of us. *"Fat Sam"* was passing the light at the end of the pier at exactly 1530.

As I entered the inner basin of the harbour I saw a familiar boat moored against the wall in the corner. It was *"Katra"* with Rod McIntosh and his wife Sandra aboard; I now knew who the lone yacht was in the early hours of the morning!

Rod and his wife are members of the club who prefer to keep their boat on the pontoons at Avoch harbour. They must have left just after midnight to be here now.

The high-sided hills around Lybster mean that radio signals are practically non-existent within the harbour area so anyone needing to contact home had to climb the steep road up to the village in order to get the use of their mobile phones.

It is a strange coincidence that the signal seems to appear right outside the nearest pub, what a hard life this is! As we are so close we might as well have a drink.

There was some kind of charity fund-raising event going on in the village and the locals were all in high spirits. It seemed only natural then that we as a club should join in. We would spend the next hour enjoying the "craic" of each others company before making our way through to in the dining room for a terrific meal.

After a couple of more beers we were all feeling the effects of such an early start and one by one made our way back to the boats.

Rod decided to make for Helmsdale to have an easier trip home the following day and we wished him luck as he sailed out of the harbour at 2030, he in turn wished us luck on our third attempt at reaching Orkney.

I was in bed by 2200.

Log Reading 4433.1 Distance today 35NM

Sunday 8th June 2003

I was awake quite early the following morning and went for a walk to loosen up the old legs, on my return I made a cup of tea and waited until there were signs of life on some of the other boats. Bill was first to stir but when the rest of them heard our conversation, you cannot talk quietly to Bill, they started to appear one by one.

The facilities at Lybster are excellent since the opening of the Heritage centre, £5 gets your boat in the harbour for the night and the use of the showers/toilets and washing machine/drier. It was on our previous visits to here that we got the idea to install similar facilities at our Tower in Cromarty.
There was a mad scramble to see who was using facilities first, the winner of course being the guy with the key in his pocket, I think that was Rod.
After everyone was suitably washed and fed the two boats that were returning to Cromarty, slipped their lines and bade us farewell and good luck for the rest of the trip.
We stood at the end of the pier and watched them round the point and went back to the quayside for a briefing on the second leg.
The plan was to sail to Wick and sit there, leaving at a time when we could hope to reach Duncansby Head at a favourable state of the tide, and this I reckoned to be at 1930.

I outlined the possible problems we could encounter in the Pentland Firth and the plan of action to cross safely.

There being no questions to the proposals, we set sail at 0830 in the direction of Wick.

The wind was the same as the day before, very light and from the SW with just a touch more south in it. We did not make much headway at all under sail and resorted to the motors again.

We arrived at Wick at around 1130, replenished our petrol tanks and filled all the spare cans we had in case we had to motor all the way.

On completion of this important task we all felt that we deserved a pint and a meal and so retired to "The Moorings" pub.

The consensus of opinion was that we leave Wick around 1530. On returning to the boats were met by the harbourmaster's assistant who agreed to waive the fees as we were only waiting for the tide.

We left at the agreed time and the wind had picked up slightly, enough to fill the spinnaker, but again without much headway. I persevered for about an hour then decided that we should press on to arrive at Duncansby Head, early, rather than late.

Bill was still having problems with his engine and to tell the truth, Gavin's was not performing at all well either. The result of this was that I reached the waypoint ten minutes ahead of Gavin and almost thirty minutes ahead of Bill.

There were lobster pots dotted around the head which gave us a good indication of the strength of the tide and Polar Wind and Fat Sam were just managing to hold station against the tide if we sat at half throttle. This way we could face back toward Wigeon and monitor his progress. We watched as he grew from a dot on the horizon to the recognisable form of a Snapdragon 21. We had started out together and we were now going to cross the dreaded Pentland Firth together. It has to be noted that we were now 45 minutes later than we had anticipated. We passed Duncansby Head at 2015.

Thanks to the lack of wind, we did not get any of the famous "overfalls" but we could plainly see all the currents and eddies that make this stretch of water one of the most dangerous in Europe.

We had studied the tidal atlas very carefully and we were able to negotiate the crossing with very little difficulty at all. However there were occasional tidal races that would pick up the boat and move it several feet in a sideways motion. This could make one feel a little concerned at first, but we seemed to get used to it quickly and soon learned to spot the dodgy bits as we approached them.

We headed in the direction of Lother Rock, with the Pentland Skerries two miles off to starboard. As one nears Lother Rock, the tide continues to take your boat and carry it midway between South Ronaldsay and the island of Swona. At this point the log on "Fat Sam" was registering 4.5 knots over the water; however the GPS showed we were doing 8.5 knots over the ground!

I felt that as Commodore, I was responsible for the safety of the crossing and I fussed about like a mother hen with the other two boats, I seemed to be getting further ahead of them all of the time and was becoming quite concerned. At one point I felt they were both too close to the island of Swona and warned them that if they did not steer toward South Ronaldsay they were in danger of the tide carrying them round North head and down to the "Merry Men of Mey".

The response I got was a change in direction from Wigeon with nothing said and a similar change of course from Polar Wind followed by a radio transmission, which I regret to say, I was unable to decipher, as Rod, it seems had finished off a bottle of wine and was quite "the merry man of Mey".

After passing the entrance to Widewall Bay, it was relatively straightforward and I rounded Hoxa Head just before 2200, here again there were lots of lobster pots, the difference here was that they had very long lines attached. I was weaving in and out of them hoping that my propeller would not foul on the ridiculously long lines. Once clear, I looked back to see the other two coming round Hoxa Head and I radioed a warning about the pots.

I sent a text message to my daughter Lynda in California to say we had successfully crossed the Pentland Firth. A few minutes later she actually phoned me to get some more details. Technology is wonderful thing; here I was sailing a little boat in Scapa Flow and talking to someone in the United States at the same time. The mind boggles.

At 2215, Steve went forward to drop the anchor in St Margaret's Hope Bay and within half an hour we were all rafted up together and having a celebratory drink, I have no idea how long we stayed up as I cannot recall going to bed. I think it's called "alcohol induced amnesia".

Log Reading 4466. 7 total distance today 33. 6 NM

Monday 9th June 2003

When I woke in the morning, I lay for a long while, in no hurry to rise. The previous two days had been quite long and I felt quite tired, even after a night's sleep. I eventually rose around 0800 and was amazed to find the cockpit strewn with empty Guinness cans and empty wine bottles. I cleared away all the rubbish and made a cup of tea during which time the gas ran out.
I inflated the rubber dinghy and went in search of somewhere to buy gas, just my luck, nearest stockist

was in Stromness. I ferried all the crews back and forth from their boats to the shore and we spent a couple of hours walking round the few shops in the town and sent some postcards home.

Eventually Neil's "nose" for finding an open hostelry was working well and upon finding the bar of the Murray Arms Hotel open and dispensing the nectar, we entered and introduced ourselves to the co-owner and barmaid, Barbara.

The bar is dotted with memorabilia of the WWII wrecks that are widely scattered in Scapa Flow and those from the scuttling of the German Fleet in WWI. There were also various pieces of diving equipment.

There was a strange object on the shelf behind the bar which, Barbara explained was to test the lung strength of divers and asked us if anyone would like to try it out. Steve and I both "smelled a rat", looked at each other and then declined. Rod and Gavin made no move to try it and Neil sat with a knowing smirk on his face. Poor old Bill unaware of what was going on said he would have a go, took a deep breath and blew into it with all the power he could muster.

A white cloud enveloped him as the rest of us fell about laughing, I think Bill was blushing, but nobody could really tell as his face was completely covered in talcum powder.

We did not stay too long in the bar, I think Bill was eager to go, and left shortly after to repeat the shore to ship transfer of personnel, then stowed away the dinghy. Once this task was completed we set sail for Stromness at 1230.

The wind was better than it had been of late, at around force 4 and although it was from the northwest and against us, we sailed up Scapa Flow. "*Polar Wind*" chose to sail to the North East of the Flow, perhaps to look at the marker buoy for the wreck of the "*Royal Oak*" which was sunk in Scapa Bay. Whatever the reason for being over there, he was chased away by the pilot boat to allow a tanker to manoeuvre. Bill was now out of sight, having pressed on again under power, as I did eventually, in order to try and restock with the gas before the shop closed.

As I motored toward Stromness Harbour, Neil came on the radio to give me directions and within ten minutes I was tied up alongside, the time was now 1650 and I had to rush to find the shop with the empty gas bottle in my hand. I made it with a couple of minutes to spare.

I wandered back to the boat, via The Royal Hotel, in time to witness "*Polar Wind*" berthing at 1800. The wind had changed and he managed to sail all the way up to the harbour entrance. Well-done Gavin! This was just as well, for he was still having problems with his engine.

I am sure the reader can guess where we went next, although I was so very tired and retired to bed at 2030, very early for me.

Log Reading 4480.5
Total distance today 13.8 NM

Tuesday 10th June 2003

I slept right through until 0815, which is very unlike me; I must have badly needed the sleep. We decided upon a rest day and stay over for another night in Stromness.

We visited Kirkwall by bus where I bought a new battery, as the old one was not holding its charge. I had a wander around the shops, stopping to buy a little something for Lilly, a little porcelain Labrador for the fireplace back home.
I wasn't being miserable; she likes that kind of thing. We had to sample a couple of the bars being as we are in the capital and then got the bus back to Stromness.

Neil and Steve decided to cook a meal for everyone, which turned out to be absolutely average. We had earlier made an arrangement with the Ferry Inn to use their shower facilities at £1.50 per head, which included the towels and we felt it was only fair that we spent some time in the bar afterwards.

Three boats in Stromness
"*Polar Wind*", "*Fat Sam*" and "*Wigeon*"

We all agreed that today had been worthwhile, as we needed the rest and with that, sat down to plan for the following day.

With Bill's continuing problem in the engine department, they planned to set out a couple of hours ahead of Gavin and me. They are also planned to go down through Gutter Sound on the inside of the island of Fara, this was a slightly shorter route and they intended dropping anchor in Long Hope Bay. There they would await the arrival of "Fat Sam" and "Polar Wind" at the Sound of Hoxa, as we intended to sail back down the Scapa Flow, where we would join up and cross the Firth again together.

After retiring to the boats we all did our own thing until it was time for bed. I am not quite sure when I turned in, but I don't suppose it really matters.

Wednesday 11th June 2003.

By the time we surfaced, Bill and Neil had gone; I think it was probably around 0630. With the problems they were having with the engine they needed to be well ahead of us.

The forecast for that day was is ideal for crossing the Pentland Firth so we are preparing for this again. After breakfast we tidied up and organised everything ready for the sail ahead.

It was 1030 when we slipped our lines and headed out into Hoy Sound.

Now it was the turn of Gavin's engine to play up, he has just informed me that he does not have any signs of water coming through the cooling jacket. Luckily the wind is sufficient to sail out of trouble, I hung about to see if they were going to be ok, they are managing fine under sail.

The tide in the sound is against us and is trying to force us out into the Atlantic, we are making a little headway but it is painfully slow. The wind is very good; we are on a reach doing 5 knots across the water but only ½ a knot across the ground.
I moved in as close to the shore as I can dare go to cut down the effect of the tide and have radioed Gavin to tell him to use this tactic.

It took almost an hour to reach Scapa Flow but by the time we did the wind had strengthened considerably and had swung round to be on our stern. We are making excellent progress now and the tide is no longer a problem.
I set a course to sail close to the "Barrel of Butter", a rock that is about one third of the way across the Flow. With Steve now at the helm, it gives me a chance to look at the charts and tidal atlas again, just to double check I have the timing right. I take a closer look at the route "*Wigeon*" plans to take and realise that at the time they intend coming out of Cantick Sound, they would run into a severe tide race with overfalls. It might be ok in light winds, but the way the wind is increasing, I think it might be

prudent to make for Widewall bay on South Ronaldsay and wait for us there. I try to radio, but can't raise them so get them on the mobile and explain the situation. I also tell them about Gavin's problem and promise to keep them up to date with events. They were going to up anchor and go to Widewall bay as I suggested.

As we approached the "Barrel of Butter" Steve was having difficulty keep us on a straight course, the boat wanted to veer off to Starboard. I reckon the wind strength to be at least a force six, gusting seven, perhaps even more!
All the diving boats are hurrying for sheltered water. I came up into the cockpit to take the helm and asked Steve to take in half of the roller reefing foresail then go forward and reef the main.
When he was at the mast taking a reef in the main I began shouting instructions to him. He glared at me and shouted "*I have only one pair of hands and I am hanging on here with my teeth*" followed by "*if you think you can do any better, get your arse up here and do it!*"

Once we had taken a full reef in the main we are still doing 7-8 knots. Steve came back to the cockpit and on seeing my face showing the obvious displeasure at his tirade of abuse, then tried to defuse the situation and he said "*sorry dad, what I meant to say was Aye Aye Skipper!*"

Bill phoned back to say they were just entering Widewall bay and that the wind was, as Bill put it, "piping up". Another call from Gavin told us that Rod had the engine in pieces in the cockpit and did not think he could rebuild it while the boat is tossing about as it is; he was however, attempting it. I asked him to keep me informed, as we had to make a decision whether or not to go for a crossing today. We also had to inform Bill and Neil what we are doing.

At 1230 Gavin radioed again to say that the task of rebuilding his outboard was impossible in these conditions, we had to find shelter to complete the job. St Margaret's Hope was probably the safest bet. I called Bill on his Mobile, telling him of the change of plans once more. They didn't sound too pleased about the whole situation but when I reminded them there was a Pub at the anchorage they quickly accepted the inevitable and up anchor once more and headed round to St Margaret's Hope Bay, a distance of around 5 miles.

Steve went forward to drop the anchor in the bay and I noted the time at 1350. Gavin and Rod got down to putting together their engine whilst Bill and Neil went off in search of a petrol station. Once all the chores were completed, petrol stowed away etc, the engine on "*Polar Wind*" was given a test run and it seemed to be ok we retired to the Murray Arms, for the now mandatory pint.

We were all back on board by 1700 and made our meals in the separate boats, exchanging the odd derogatory remark to each other across the water, there being only 35 to 40 feet between each of the craft.

We had a party aboard tonight with Gavin bringing the bottle of gin that had been left on board the boat when he bought "*Polar Wind*". There were copious amounts of the said gin, lager, export and Guinness dispatched and our hearty laughter must have sounded strange to the landlubbers ashore.

When it came time to retire I was quite surprised that Gavin and Rod did not end up capsizing their dinghy on the way back to their own boat. Rod finished off the evening by emptying his bladder at the bow of their boat whilst yelling his undying love for the barmaid in the "Murray".

The last sentence is not strictly the truth, but it's near enough. If I were to relate what he actually was shouting, I am sure that would render both him and me liable to criminal proceedings.

Log Reading 4493.9
Total distance today 13.4 NM

Thursday 12th June 2003

Wind was very light again this morning and was forecast to be variable 2-3. I checked my calculation again in the morning and determined that the best time for us to enter the firth was 1530. We had breakfast, put away the inflatable and decided to sail round to Widewall Bay where we could wait for the time to pass.

An hour later we were tucked inside Widewall Bay, by this time the wind had really dropped to no more than a whisper and we rafted all three boats on one anchor and sat down to discuss the meaning of life!

We also discussed Bill's engine and decided to take a closer look at it. One Spark plug had signs that it not been working at all so another was fitted and Bingo! It is now firing on **two** cylinders.
The next hour was spent "ribbing" Bill and exhausting every imaginable pun, much to the annoyance of Bill until he said, "OK, enough is enough!" So we then dropped the subject.

With the wind now gone completely, I figured we could leave now at 1500 so off we went; "*Wigeon*" had the bow wave of a destroyer.

Round two of the sick jokes and puns now that we are out of his reach.

Rafted up in Widewall Bay (Polar Wind taking Photo)

The crossing today was flat calm, just as it was going the other way on Sunday, Gavin gave us a call on the radio at one point to say that they had spotted a killer whale of the south tip of South Ronaldsay, we looked back were unable to see it.
I was reading 5 knots on the log and 9 knots over the ground and in no time at all we were passing Duncansby Head.

We reached Noss Head at 1830 and eventually sailed into Wick for 1930.
We ended up in "Camps" bar where a Karaoke was in full swing but a quick look round the bar gave an

indication of the class of clientele. Some of them looked and acted like extras from the film "Deliverance",
So much so I requested "Duelling Banjos", if you haven't seen the film you won't find that funny. We stayed for a little while but soon got fed up and headed back to the boats.

I was in bed by 2230.

Log Reading 4515.2
Total distance today 21.3 NM

Friday 13th June 2003

Everyone was up and about for 0700 and we were anxious to get on our way. Steve was leaving today to get a bus to Inverness, as he has to get back down the road to fly out on Royal Navy duties to some far-flung region to, as he puts it *"protect the sovereignty of our country so you lazy b******s can sleep easy at night"*.

I now have to sail single handed on the way home.

We wasted a lot of time getting more petrol and having to go up to harbour office to pay the dues of £11.75 each for one night.
By the time we sailed out of the harbour it was after 0930. We had lost half the tide and although we

were making good time at the start we soon slowed as the tide weakened its influence in our direction. The wind was straight on the nose and although it had been forecast to be 3-4, it was a lot stronger than that. There was quite a heavy sea running and I had a fully reefed main and only half the foresail out, sailing close-hauled. God this is hard work.

By the time we got to Clythe Head the tide had turned against us and the wind was now in excess of force 7 probably nearer 8. The waves were pounding against my bows and every time I got some headway a wave would hit the boat and stop it almost completely. I sailed for a good while but could see that the relative bearing on Clythe Ness Lighthouse was remaining the same I decided to go on power. This too proved to be extremely difficult. I could hear Gavin on the radio but I could not let go the helm. I was to find out later that he was asking if we should pull into Lybster for a spot of lunch! The wind is ferocious now; the only thing the forecast got right today was the bloody date!

It took me over three hours to go the 2 miles from Clythe Ness to Lybster and the wind is still increasing.

I was very, very glad to get into Lybster at 1430.

Sat in the pub (where else would one go?) and discussed the plan for tomorrow, if the wind has dropped sufficiently we will leave very early and try to get all the way home, if it is still windy we will settle for Helmsdale. Bill volunteered to get up at the crack of dawn and if conditions are right, we will make as early a start as we can.

Did not have much to drink tonight, as we are all pooped and ready for going home.

I can't remember what time I went to bed but it was early.

Log Reading 4527.9
Total distance today 12.7NM

Saturday 14th June 2003.

Bill duly arose as first light came in and seeing that the wind had dropped completely, woke the rest of us. I noted a forecast from the radio of "winds light and variable, 1-2". What a country we live in. It's either blowing so hard, the seagulls are flying backwards, or there is no wind at all!

We were all washed and fed and on our way by 0515, a good time as the tide was against us, but was almost spent. In another hour it will be in our favour.

We resigned ourselves to the fact that we are going to spend another day under power and set a course for home. The good thing about this kind of weather and having to motor when I am sailing single-handed it is a simple task to put the kettle on for a "brew", but to tell the truth it is an extremely boring way of making headway.

With the navigation being so simple in these conditions, I tend to become a bit complacent about taking a fix or an estimated position, as these are very familiar waters to me. I was relaxing at the helm watching the world go by when I was interrupted by the sound of Bill's voice on the VHF, pointing out that he was running short of fuel. *"Polar Wind"* responded by suggesting we head for Portmahomack to replenish our supplies.

I then suggested that the easiest option lay with calling in to Helmsdale, as the tide would be fine for entering. This was unanimously agreed upon and the radios fell silent for a while. About ten minutes later I heard Rod saying *"Fat Sam, where are you going"? "Helmsdale of course,"* I replied, *"what's that off to starboard then?"* Asked Rod. *"Berriedale"* said I with indignant confidence. *"I think not!"* was the cheeky reply.

I got out my binoculars and looked at the town 2 miles off to starboard, My God! It is Helmsdale! I will never be allowed to live this down.

Rather than engage in further conversation, to make excuses would have been futile, I simply altered course by 90 degrees to starboard and followed the transit line into the harbour.

Any thoughts that they would be sympathetic and not raise the subject were quickly dispelled when they appeared in the harbour entrance behind me. Let's just say they gave me a lot of stick and Rod and Gavin still make the odd snide remark about this episode to this day.

We quickly filled the cans with petrol and were back aboard the boats inside half an hour. We took a further fifteen minutes to make a cup of soup and a buttered roll, and then headed back out into the Moray Firth at 0945.

There was still insufficient wind to sail, so we continued to motor toward Tarbet Ness, Bill was obviously more confident with the extra petrol onboard and was well ahead of the others by the time we reached the Lighthouse at Tarbet Ness.

Shortly after I passed the point the wind got up from the north east and I was able to fly the spinnaker again this lasted until I was just passing the "*Three Kings*" cardinal mark.

Jock Wingate in "*Heart of Gold*" had come out to meet us and was sailing at first, but as he reached me at the cardinal mark, the wind died, both he and I took down our sails to motor yet again. The tide had turned some time ago and the ebb was pushing us back.

As I passed between the Sutors, there was a sudden squall that brought with it a good wind, which I could have used to enter Cromarty with a blaze of glory with all sails up. To tell the truth I could not be bothered and in any case, no one would have noticed. I carried on with the motor for the last mile home.

It was a great feeling to have achieved our goals; an even greater feeling was spending the night in my own bed.

Log Reading   4560.0
Total distance today   32.1 NM
Total Distance covered for the trip 161.90 NM

Again I competed in Moray Firth Cruiser Race and several regattas, bringing a very satisfying end to the season.

At the end of that season in the month of October, I stepped down as Commodore, a position I had held for a full eight years. I felt I had done my bit and looked forward to taking it easy for a while and concentrating more on my sailing.
Gavin Meldrum was elected in my place and I became the club's first Rear Commodore

Sailing now is No. 1 again

2004

Whilst out sailing one Sunday on the Cromarty Firth I became involved in an unofficial race with a couple of the other boats from Cromarty Club. My regular crew, of Jean-Yves Lemel and Claire Cadet, affectionately known as the *"French Connection"* were actually sailing the boat as I *supervised* with the mandatory G&T in my hand. When something out of the ordinary happened...

Mishap on the water
On Sunday the eleventh July Whilst in a yachting race,
My Boat "Fat Sam" was at the front setting a cracking pace,
When suddenly without a warning, one of my trusty crew,
Did something of a Faux Pas, which came from out of the Blue.

The crewmember in question is our own Femme de France,
And what she did to hold us up gave the other boats a chance,
She seemed to grab the "whisker pole" and throw it over the side,
The initial thought that crossed my mind one of homicide!

Anyone who knows me well, Sait that I'm no killer,
In an effort to recover it, I then took over the tiller,
I turned the boat completely round to retrieve that,
which was lost,
Knowing in my heart of hearts how much this move
would cost.

To witness our predicament, filled the other boats
with mirth,
Watching "Fat Sam" motionless au milieu du Firth,
We caught up with the missing pole, luckily still
floating,
Just as "Norseman" sailed right past (I'm sure I saw
him gloating!)

They say it's not the winning; it's just the taking
part,
But when you lose a lead like that, you tend to lose
some heart,
To harbour any resentment, would certainly be
unfair,
And it's Difficile to hold a grudge against a girl like
Claire,

When the race was finally over and the calculations
done,
Then checked against the handicaps to see just who
had won,
It will come as no real great surprise to learn it
wasn't me!

How do I feel on hindsight? You've guessed it...C'est la Vie.

You will of course have noticed that I have exercised some poetic license during the composure of this rhyme

George Selvester 13th July 2004

Westward Ho!

The idea of a "staggered" cruise to the west coast, starting one weekend, leaving the boats at a point, picking them up and continuing the cruise the following week, was first raised in a pub in Fort William during the 2002 Great Glen Cruise.

It was again discussed on our return from the successful 2003 cruise to Orkney, and the idea seemed to gain momentum.
It was unfortunate for Gavin Meldrum, that on his election to Commodore in October of 2003, the destination of his first Cruise as leader had, in effect, already been made!

After seeing the support for the idea, Gavin conceded that the 2004 Commodore's Cruise should be an attempt to sail round the island of Mull to visit places such as "*Fingal's Cave*" and "*Tinker's Hole*".

129

Preparations were soon underway to make this, the best-attended cruise to date.

After several meetings to discuss the logistics of transporting crews to and from the halfway point and the probable number of boats taking part, the business of planning the actual cruise was set about. Relying heavily on the experience of Jock Wingate, the idea of sailing round Mull was discarded, as many of the crews intending to take part were still a little "green" for such an undertaking, and a more realistic plan was to take each day as it came, after taking into account the weather and the distances between the selected ports.

Gavin spent a great deal of time and effort putting every possible detail down in writing and distributing all relevant information to the skippers committed to taking part, without this commitment, the cruise would not have enjoyed the success that it did.

However, *"The best laid plans of mice and men aft gang aglay"*, even after all the efforts by our Commodore, the plans started to fray a little at the edges. This was due to three main reasons.
Firstly: the "non conformists" who appear in all walks of life upsetting the harmony of the majority. *Cromarty Boat Club has its fair share of those people,* those who do their own thing no matter what.

Secondly: some members were overtaken by circumstances and were forced into making decisions they would not normally have made. Thirdly: work commitments meant that some had to be home earlier than they would really have wanted and altered the finish date to suit.

All of these points led to the cruise fragmenting into three separate groups, although it has to be said that on the whole it was an enjoyable experience.

The following is a personal account of the trip, peppered as usual by my dubious wit and sometimes-vitriolic comments, I will apologise in advance to anyone who may feel I have offended him or her.

George Selvester,
Rear Commodore,

The transfer.

Many skippers and crews, myself included, had only time enough for one week per year dedicated to cruising their boat. Those skippers agreed to sail their boats as far as Corpach on the week prior to the official cruise date and duly set off on Friday 18th June.

They were:

Norseman: Peter Baxter and Lorraine Beigley
Tunnag: Bill Paterson and Alex Davidson
Polar Wind: Gavin Meldrum and Davy Hamilton
Fat Sam: George Selvester and Martin McPherson
Wigeon: Mike   Holmes   and   Jock   Wingate*
Pugster: Pug Peterson and John Rahtz
Sun Sieray: Mike   Wilson,   Jean-Yves   Lemel   and
Claire Cadet

As well as one late addition, Ron King.

*As far as Inverness

Friday 18th June 2004.

0900: Log reading 4754.4:   Wind   Light   and
variable

We   left   Cromarty   in   company   with   *"Tunnag"*,
"Norseman"   and   *"Polar Wind"*   to   be   joined   at
Fortrose by *"Sun Sieray"*.
"Pugster" had left at around 0600 and *"Wigeon"* had
left at 0800.
It was agreed we would all meet up in the Muirton
Basin.

My   brother-in-law,   Martin,   was   looking   forward   to
the trip round to Inverness as he had only been as
far as Cromarty Bank buoy in the past.
Once we rounded the South Sutor under power, the
wind rose a little from the North East to around a

132

force 4 and allowed me to carry a spinnaker on a bit of a reach. We began to make excellent time and showed 5-6 knots on the log, which is faster than we could achieve under power.

"*Fat Sam*" managed to overtake "*Tunnag*" just as we passed below the radio mast at Eathie, making us the lead boat of our group and in no time at all we were passed Fort George, the tide was also helping us, the GPS registering 7-8 knots over ground.

When we passed the Chanonry Light I called on the VHF for "*Sun Sieray*" to tell them to come out and meet us, Claire answered informing us that they had been requested, by mobile phone, to await the arrival of Iso Meldrum. Mike then came on air explaining that she was bringing the charts that a forgetful Gavin had left behind. The Commodore had obviously wanted to keep this quiet and Mike had just broadcast the oversight to the whole fleet.

The wind continued in our favour and I could carry the spinnaker until just before the Kessock Bridge when we were hit by a sudden squall.

With the boat in the middle of a broach, Martin discovered that the colour of adrenalin is brown.

I had to go forward to lower the halyard but with the boat lying at an angle of 45 degrees, this is not an easy task, the damned thing had a knot in it, which I found difficult to undo. Martin was yelling at me to cut it, which I of course refused to do, *it was well and truly jammed!* After a few well chosen swear words and a lot of physical persuasion, I eventually managed to free off the halyard and drop the whole lot into the water, allowing the boat to sit upright, before recovering it on board.

When I got back to the cockpit, I found that Martin was a peculiar shade of chewing gum grey and shaking like a leaf. I apologised for giving him such a fright, explaining that we had been in no real danger, or I would have cut it.
Martin is still convinced that the boat was completely on its side and that I am some sort of head case.

It is true that I sometimes forget that with years of experience under my belt, what I think as a little bit uncomfortable on the boat, others may think of as being their worst nightmare.
I figured that the least I said at the moment the sooner he would feel better and we motored the last mile to the Clachnaharry sea lock in relative silence. The time now was 1245

"*Wigeon*" had arrived about 30 minutes in front of us and was waiting in the lock for us. Once our paperwork was completed we moved up to above the works lock then four of us adjourned to the local inn for a pub lunch and waited for the others to catch up.

When I walked back down after lunch to see the others in the works lock, I learned that "*Sun Sieray*" had experienced problems with their engine and had managed to raise a sail in an effort to get out of trouble. Unfortunately they collided with: first the sea wall, and then the lock gates. They were still outside the sea lock waiting for an engine from somewhere or other.

It surprised me that one of his crew, Ron King, had jumped ship at the first sign of trouble and was now aboard "*Polar Wind*" muttering something about it not being his problem.

It would appear that he left the others just when he was most needed.

Gavin was explaining to me the rough details of "*Sun Sieray's*" mishap, when Ron shouted up to me "*It's me George, I am a Jonah*", to which of course I replied "*You'll get no argument from me on that one*".

We all, with the exception of Mike, made our way into Muirton Basin to meet up with "*Pugster*". Jock had arranged for all the boats to be put up the flight together at around 1400.

Alastair Stewart appeared on the scene to wish us all luck and when he heard of Mike's predicament went to offer his assistance, as any true friend would. He eventually found a second hand engine for a good price and Mike's damaged engine was sent to Caley Marina for repair.

I admire Mike for his spirit to continue and although he ended up being an hour behind us he and the "French Connection" would eventually catch up with us in Fort Augustus.

The locking up through the Muirton flight went without a hitch and Tomnahurich bridge; Dochgarroch and Dochfour were soon behind us. All five boats entered Loch Ness at 1710.
By now the wind had dropped to no more than a whisper, with the rain falling steadily and heavily.

Just prior to the trip I had spent four days in hospital with a damaged right elbow, which had developed an infection, but because I had been looking forward to this trip for so long, I was determined not to miss it and although I promised myself I would take it easy and not exert myself too much, it is not all that easy when there is so much to do on the boat.
The work I had just put my arm through for the past eight hours was now beginning to tell. It had now swollen up again and was very painful. As the engine was now doing all the work and Martin was at the helm, it gave me a chance to rest it for a while.

The remainder of the journey down Loch Ness was dismal to say the least; we were both very cold, wet and in my case, depressed, not helped at all by the pain in my arm, and the rain was never-ending.

It was a welcoming sight indeed, to see the Fort Augustus approach light loom up out of the murk.

At 2115, I was securing "*Fat Sam*" alongside a pontoon below the locks. In a matter of minutes I had locked the boat up and we were on our way to the Lock Inn for a bite to eat and a pint of Guinness, in Martin's case, a Vodka and coke. We ate garlic bread and a plate of chips washed down by another drink and the heat of the room soon brought us back to a comfortable feeling of contentment.

At 2200 Jean-Yves and Claire came into the bar to let us know that the last remaining boat of the fleet had finally made it into port. We stayed for another drink and enjoyed the banter of the crews in the smoke-free atmosphere of the upstairs lounge for an additional half an hour.

The efforts of the day had caught up with us; Martin & I decided to retire at 2230 and sneaked off to our beds for a well-deserved nights sleep.

Log Reading: 4787.6

Total distance covered today: 33.2 NM

Saturday 19th June 1004

I rose at around 0730 and went straight to the shower block, emerging after 20 minutes, feeling a whole lot better than I had the night before.
I was still taking antibiotics for the infection in my arm, but felt today that I did not need any painkillers.

Back at the boat Martin was up and he too went for a shower, whilst I made the breakfast of boiled eggs, tea and bread.
A quick meeting of the boat owners, at which Gavin suggested that because of the long day yesterday we should take it easier today and take the later lock up the flight at 1100.
Everyone agreed with this suggestion and set about replenishing water and fuel for the next part of the journey.

Martin had made arrangements with his church to be on duty as mini-bus driver and to help with the communion on Sunday and had to be off the boat sometime today. He went off in search of a timetable for the Citylink coach service to Inverness, returning after 15 minutes to say he could get one at 0940.
He was disappointed at having to leave me and wished now that he had told the church he was busy, he obviously got over his little fright of the previous day, as he wanted to continue the

adventure. I told him there would be another time and at 0930 walked up to the bus stop with him to see him off. I had enjoyed his company for the start of trip and looked forward to him sailing with me again.

The fleet enter the lock at Fort Augustus

With me now being crew-less, Claire Cadet volunteered to help the old man with the sore arm, I readily agreed. We entered the bottom lock just after 1030 and were all clear of the top lock by midday.

Bill Paterson had discovered the night before that he had a leaking fuel tank and having removed it, went off in search of a garage to have it braised. The rest of the gang brought his boat up the flight whilst he was gone and by the time we reached the top he returned with the repaired tank. He was only ten minutes behind us by the time he had fitted the tank and as we were going that bit slower, he caught up with us before the next lock at Kytra

It was now plain sailing, rather motoring, to get through the Cullochy Lock and into Loch Oich, I was a fair bit ahead of the rest by the time we reached the **Great Glen Water Park** and I tied up to the pontoons to await the rest before going through the Laggan swing bridge.

"Pugster" was next to arrive and was coming in to the pontoon a bit too quickly, with John at the helm. I went round to fend him off and hurt my arm yet again. When all the other boats arrived, someone suggested that we go to the pub here at the park; as there was no opposition to this suggestion, off we went.

An hour later, we were on our way again, but the decision had been made only to go as far as Laggan Locks. Jock Wingate had left "*Wigeon*" at Inverness, Mike Holmes had brought the boat down from there single-handed and Nick Owens would now join him for the final stage. Nick sorted out his radio problem so we could now communicate with them via VHF.

The Inn on the Water is an Old Dutch barge named "*Eagle*" the proprietor is a strange character with even stranger political convictions. I would say he stands slightly to the right of Genghis Khan. He makes Margaret Thatcher seem like a Socialist.

I will not say I did not like him, but he will not be on my Christmas card list. He did make the effort to rustle up a seafood platter for all the crews at short notice and the surroundings inside the barge are very homely and comfortable.
I enjoyed my food and although there was no Guinness available, I had a couple of bottles of stout. After a while my arm began to hurt again so I went to bed at around 2200.

Log Reading 4794.0

Total distance covered today 6.4 NM

Sunday 20th June 2004.

With most of the crews showered, shaved, shampooed and shhh!
We don't say that word in good log accounts, we were ready for the off at 0900.

Loch Lochy was beautiful with hardly a ripple on the water, there was a very slight breeze coming from the north but when I tried to use the spinnaker it would barely fill and registered no speed at all on the log.

As we had to get to Banavie by around midday we had to press on with the "*five horses of the Suzuki*".
A fairly uneventful trip from there to Banavie through the two locks and a swing bridge at Gairlochy and Claire and I discussed many topics from religion to Scottish history.
Claire did all the helming whilst I sat like a gentleman sailor drinking gin and tonic; medicinal, as I need it for the Quinine in the tonic, for the mosquitoes!

On arrival at the top of Neptune's Staircase we made all the boats secure and retired to the comfort of "The Moorings" bar.
This is a very strange bar and seems to try to dissuade the like of me for a more upmarket clientele. They insist of serving you at the table, *for a pint of Guinness for goodness sake.*

Gavin had arranged for the transport in the shape of: Iso Meldrum, with a 4X4, Greta Young with her 4X4 and Andy Young with his estate car. They all did an excellent job, for which I give my thanks.

In no time at all we were back home to start work on the Monday morning. The only thing that would keep me going this week is the thought of starting the real cruise next Friday/Saturday.

During the week after we returned home, the others in the club were to set out as and when they could to congregate at the Corpach Lock on the Friday evening.

"*Tunnag*", "*Pugster*" and "*Sun Sieray*" had all gone out into Loch Linnhe for a few days ending up at Loch Crerran. They had agreed to meet up with "*Heart of Gold*" and "*Kismet*"(who were leaving Cromarty together on the Tuesday afternoon) sometime late on the Thursday or early Friday to take the boats that were left at Banavie down Neptune's staircase.

Gus Ferguson in "*Oran Anna*" was unsure of when he would be setting off but assured us he would be there at the appointed time

I was driving the service bus to and from Inverness and was hoping to monitor their progress as they made their way through the Inverness Firth to Clachnaharry. This was not to be, I never even caught the slightest glimpse any of them. I did however; get a call from Gavin to tell me that they were safely into the canal system before the storm, which was forecast to be with us for the remainder of the week from Wednesday onwards.

"*Pio Moso*", one of the Invergordon boats taking part in the cruise left his mooring early on the Wednesday morning and he too managed to enter the canal before the weather broke.

The last boat to leave, another from Invergordon, was "*Far Enuff*", skippered by Danny Coutts, was not quite so lucky. As I was leaving Cromarty, driving the 1140 to Inverness, I saw him making heavy weather against a very strong easterly wind, which was a force seven touching eight and forecast to worsen.

I called Gavin on his mobile to tell him I saw Danny as he passed the Natal Buoy. Gavin informed me that he had already had a conversation with him and that he (Danny) intended to see what the Inverness Firth was like and if too bad, would abort the trip.

I was to learn later that when "*Far Enuff*" turned into the Inverness Firth, the wind, now being from his stern, was so bad that he had no option but to carry on to the Sea Loch at Clachnaharry. Apparently the seas were breaking over his stern and regularly filling the cockpit. I would think he would have given a sigh of relief when he entered the lock at around 1500. All the boats were now in the canal system for the planned assembly at Corpach.

Menno and Jane with "*Wapiti*" were already moored at Caley Marina and would set off down the canal to join the rest whenever they could.

1st phase successfully completed.

The Actual Cruise

Friday 25th June 2004.

I had taken an extra day holiday so that we could travel down today to be ready for the off first thing on the Saturday morning, which was the official start date of the cruise.

Lilly was working this morning and I made all the arrangements for our bus trip to Corpach. Most of our gear had been left on the boat last week so we were travelling light. I received a phone call in the morning to tell me that Andy needed something taken down to Corpach and that Greta would drop it off before we caught the bus from Cromarty at 1340. She arrived at around 1300 with a holdall full of groceries for Andy so I am not travelling light after all, but he would do the same for me.

We had arranged a couple of days earlier to meet Peter and Lorraine in Inverness for a drink, this we did at "Shots" bar at 1600. We sat there until ten minutes before the City-Link bus was due to leave then wandered round to the bus station and boarded with a few minutes to spare before departure. The journey to Fort William only takes a couple of hours, being an employee of the bus company has certain advantages and we were taken back to the depot when the driver had finished and dropped off right next to Neptune's staircase.

A quick phone call to Gavin let us know they were in a pub called "The "Trade Winds", we stopped a woman walking her dog who told us it is only quarter of a mile away along the main road.
A full mile later, with all of us with sore feet and exhausted from carrying all our gear we arrived at the boats never having passed the pub. I bet her ears were burning!

It was great to see a total of fourteen boats from our club all gathered in the basin; there were also two from Avoch, "*Lyrebird*" and "*Katra*".

There was a party in full swing aboard "Wapiti" but I deliberately avoided it, as there is nothing worse than trying to get into a party mood when everyone around has been at it for hours and you are starting from cold.

By the time Lilly and I had sorted out the bedding and stowed away all the other gear we had a couple of drinks with Peter and Lorraine then went off to our beds.

The Fleet assembled at Corpach basin

Saturday 26th June 2004.

Today was to be the start of the official cruise but when I went up to the shower block I met Bill Paterson coming back clutching a weather report he had just received from the Lock Keeper: winds forecast for today in excess of force nine.

He was off to Gavin's boat to relay the information, I don't think we need a meeting for this, we have to stay put today to see if it is a better outlook tomorrow. The last thing I want is to sicken Lilly on the first day. I have spent several years trying to persuade her to join me on my annual cruise and now that she has agreed I want to look after her so she will come again.

The day was spent at the local shops and of course the pub but before the day was over I would be suffering from *harbour rot* and desperate to get away from here, even if it meant going back up the canal in the direction of home. All in all it was a totally wasted day.

The evening brought a little cheer that had the effect of making feel at ease again, Peter and Lorraine had invited us aboard "*Norseman*" for an evening meal of steaks with onions and potatoes. It was delicious. It's amazing how the girls can adapt to such cramped conditions and still serve up a decent meal. The meal was followed by? You guessed it, gins and tonic. We were later joined by Jock Wingate and spent the rest of the evening with Jock and I trying to outdo each other with our tall tales of our sailing experiences, we even touched on our time in the services with loads of anecdotes and ribald stories which probably bored the pants of the girls, metaphorically speaking, of course.

The really annoying thing now is of course that the wind strength had never reached anywhere near what had been forecast, we could have been out of here and down Loch Linnhe a fair bit to Loch Creran or some other sheltered spot in that vicinity.

However I suppose these things are sent to try us. I tried not to dwell on it, as it would only have made me depressed, after all tomorrow is another day.

Eventually it was time for bed, don't ask me what time it was, I have no idea.

Sunday 27th June 2004

I awoke at 0630 and decided to get cleaned up as early as possible, to avoid the rush; I collected my things and went off to the shower block arriving just as Alex was emerging from the shower room; we discussed the weather outlook and both agreed that we had to get away today.

When in the shower I noticed that had had some sort of rash round about my hips, I thought perhaps the famous "Highland Midge" had got inside my sleeping bag during the night and had a feast of me.

Once finished, I walked round to the Lock Keeper's office to get a weather report: Wind SW force 4-5 gusting 6 and yes, more rain.

I passed the information onto Gavin, who said we would have a skippers' meeting at 0900 to discuss the day's plan of action.

After breakfast I told Peter that I had been bitten my midges during the night and he suggested, jokingly, that it might have been fleas. Whatever it was, I put my sleeping bag out and aired it by hanging it over the boom.

The skippers' meeting duly took place at the prescribed time and the suggestion that we go to Port Appin, was dismissed in favour of Loch Aline. Although this is a fair distance to go for one day, especially against the wind, the general opinion was that it would better to push on as we had already lost one day.

We "locked in" to the sea lock at 1000 where there were a couple of mishaps. Mike Holmes, with "*Wigeon*" had a problem when a gust of wind caught the boat as they were leaving and managed to strike the outside wall, with a sickening crunch, as he went out.

"*Favour*" with Bob Evans as skipper and a crew of Bill Graham and Ron King, somehow managed to let go the stern line long before they should have, the boat ended up swinging wildly out of control.

In an effort to arrest this they grabbed "*Pio Moso*", which being tied to "*Fal Sant*", then involved me in the circus! I had great difficulty holding my boat in position and was almost pulled over the side at one point.

It is the first time I have ever seen a boat leaving a lock going astern.

Aware of the identities of those aboard "*Favour*", I am sure any club member reading this can speculate as to which one was dumb enough to let go the line.

I can forgive Mike Holmes for any errors he might make, being new to sailing; he is on a very steep learning curve. Others, however, who *claim* to have years of sailing experience, should not be making basic mistakes such as I have witnessed recently.

By 1030 we cleared the lock and motored out into Loch Linnhe, I felt a lot safer now that we had plenty sea room to avoid the unexpected actions of irresponsible individuals. With the wind, as promised, very brisk, straight on the nose and with the flood tide against us, progress was slow but steady, once past the Corran Narrows, the wave pattern increased in intensity and size, making headway uncomfortable.

"*Wapiti*" was heard on the VHF informing us of their decision to make for the shelter of Ballachulish Bay and wished the rest of the fleet all the best for the remainder of our trip. Shortly after that "*Pio Moso*" radioed to say he was making for Kentallen Bay for but would attempt to catch us up when the weather abated slightly.

Bill Paterson had already made up his mind that he would be returning a couple of days earlier than originally planned. I had felt from the early stages of the planning that if he stayed down a full week prior to us arriving on Friday 25th that he would be more or less "spent" and would want to get home early. This theory was quickly confirmed when "*Tunnag*", expressing similar feelings to those of "*Pio Moso*" called to say "*there is no way I am punching my way through this to do it all again on the way back tomorrow*". He too, then made for Kentallen Bay.

At one point the constant pitching and tossing got to me, I did not feel very well and could not understand why. Lilly was also getting a bit fed up, so it was my turn to contact Gavin to tell him I was heading for Port Appin for the night, "*Wigeon*" intimated that he would follow me in.

The way things were going you would probably have got good odds from the bookies on no boats at all reaching Loch Aline

As I approached the south end of the island of Shuna, I could see "*Sun Sieray*" heading north; I contacted him on Channel six to ask what he was doing.

He said he was trying to meet up with the rest of the fleet. I told him that the majority of the fleet were South of his present position and that he should turn around and head the other way. He was worried that his depth sounder was only showing 1.5m of water under his boat. I assured him that the sounder must be faulty as he was in safe water.

I then overheard "*Kismet*" telling "*Norseman*" that the wind had eased slightly and that making headway had become less traumatic.

I then weighed up the pros and cons of our present situation.

1. The wind direction for staying at Port Appin is not ideal.
2. Mike Wilson could benefit for having my experience to help him.
3. The wind is easing slightly; the trip would be a little less uncomfortable.
4. I would like to stick to the plan of action decided upon this morning

Something, on which Gavin was later to comment, was that as I had no Guinness on board "*Fat Sam*" I needed to keep up with him to help consume some of his supply.

I consulted Lilly with all these facts and she left the decision up to me. I still did not feel too great, but after speaking to Mike Holmes in "*Wigeon*" again, we carried on in a southerly direction.

I tried a couple of times to carry a foresail but it is proved fruitless with the wind from dead ahead. The wind had risen again making the journey seem longer than it actually was even with the tide now in our favour. By now I now felt terrible, cold, tired and very listless.

After rounding the point into the Sound of Mull I slowed down to let "*Wigeon*" and "*Sun Sieray*" catch up so that they could follow me into Loch Aline. Mike Wilson expressed his gratitude, saying that he was having difficulty with his navigation.

"*Wigeon*" managed to run out of fuel in mid channel when entering Loch Aline but "*Sun Sieray*" was close enough to pass him a spare gallon to get him in. His inexperience of all things to do with cruising is fairly obvious, why did he not ensure he had enough fuel for this leg?
I am sure he will learn valuable lessons from this trip!

Once inside the confines of the small loch I steered toward the cluster of moorings in the southwest corner of the bay, Gavin indicated that we could raft to "*Polar Wind*" for the night, an invitation I gladly accepted and was alongside by 1700.
With everything secured, I sat down to relax for a bit but found that I was shivering uncontrollably and felt very cold and not at all well, I refused the offer of something to eat and *also refused a Guinness*, I must be dying!

I went straight into my sleeping bag and went to sleep.

Log Reading: 4837.6

Total distance covered today 31.6NM

Monday 28th June 2004.

I awoke at around 0700 to discover my whole body was covered in a horrid rash that was extremely irritating. After a bit of breakfast I motored over to "*Norseman*" to consult with our resident physician. In no time at all he diagnosed that I had eaten or drunk something to which I had developed an allergy. Lilly thought it was the chemicals in the purifying tablets used in the fresh water tanks of the boat.
He supplied me with hydrocortisone cream and anti-histamine tablets which began working soon after.

The use of the outboard for most of the day down Loch Linnhe had all but exhausted my fuel stocks. I headed for the little jetty next to the ferry terminal and walked up to the filling station at the top of the hill with the three empty cans. On my way past the two Mikes, who had their boats rafted up together, I had told them what I was doing and as we had already agreed we would be setting off at 0930, I suggested that they too replenish their fuel supplies.
It was now 0830 and the shop/filling station had just opened for business.
It took me over half an hour to complete the task, get back on board and return to my berth alongside "*Polar Wind*".
Neither of the two Mikes had yet made a move to get fuel, perhaps the two "novices" will in time realise the importance of being prepared in plenty of

time when cruising/sailing. I thought by now that the caustic comments I am guilty of making in such circumstances would have brought the message home.

But, as they say "it takes all kinds to make a world".

"*Oran Anna*" had been at the jetty at the time I was getting my petrol and had now disappeared; presumably they had gone ahead but did not communicate their intentions before leaving.

"*Heart of Gold*" left on time with "*Kismet*", "*Norseman*" and "*Fat Sam*" close behind, Gavin said we should just press on and he would bring up the rear, escorting the stragglers.

As the leading boats re-entered the Sound of Mull we heard "*Pio Moso*" telling us he could see our sails from his position further to the east. He had spent the night at Northern end of the island of Shuna at a little sheltered marina and had left early, hoping to rendezvous with us; he is now only two miles behind and should meet with Gavin as he comes out into the Sound.

The wind was a bit "fluky" for the first hour, with a mix of sailing and motoring, by the time I reached the light on **Eilean Glas** the wind had picked up to the forecast strength of 4-5 and was giving me a perfect *reach* up the remainder of the Sound of Mull.

"*Pugster*", with no crew aboard, had been under power all the time on since leaving Corpach in no time at all his powerful 22hp diesel left us in his wake.

"*Kismet*" leaving Loch Aline

At 1230 just as I was entering Tobermory Bay, Gus, in "*Oran Anna*" sailed past me to tell me that they were now heading homeward as both he and his crew had important business to attend to at home and needed all the time to get through the canal. I wished them *Bon Voyage* and said I would see them when we got home ourselves.

I could now see "*Heart of Gold*", "*Pugster*" and "*Kismet*" having already picked up a mooring each quite close to the shore. I contacted Jock for permission to *lie alongside.*

From this mooring, could see "*Far Enuff*" tied up to a pontoon and tried to speak to him via the VHF, to find out the cost involved. Unable to contact him by this means, I opted instead to phone him, by this time he had cast off but told us that the berth was paid for using an honesty box sited at the end of the pontoon, Jock and I quickly moved our boats to the space he had just vacated.

The rest of the fleet arrived at intervals over the next hour; I could now see the familiar shape and colour of Danny's boat returning to the pontoon with "*Pio Moso*" in tow.
Danny is Cox of the Invergordon lifeboat when at home and it now seems as if he on a "busman's holiday" having to rescue another stricken vessel. As it was, it had only broken a shear pin on the outboard.
With "*Pio Moso*" now safely alongside Danny once more motored off heading for Oban. He would have liked to stay with us but had an important hospital appointment on the Thursday.

Lilly and I went ashore to do some shopping at the local Co-op, have a look round the town and put the provisions back aboard the boat before meeting up with some of the other crews in the Mish Nish Hotel, where Gavin and Rod had managed to arrange the use of a shower.
Just our luck, we have arrived here ten minutes after they stop serving lunch.

We all discussed our next move over a pint or two and agreed that the original plan of spending the night in Loch Droma Bhuidhe seemed a good idea and returned to the boats at 1615 to continue our journey, picking up a bag of fish and chips on the way, from a chip van situated at the top of the pier.

Gavin contacted the crews aboard *"Favour", "Sun Sieray"* and *"Wigeon"* who had all opted to remain here, preferring the fleshpots of Tobermory to the seclusion of our chosen destination.

The wind had backed slightly since lunchtime and allowed us to reach across to Auliston Point and a run into the narrow entrance to the loch.
By 1730 all the boats had dropped anchor within a few metres of each other, we discussed the possibility of a barbecue on the beach but the return of the rain soon scuppered that idea.
I had a few gins and tonic and Guinness; Lilly had vodka and coke whilst we both watched Rod trying to fish of the stern of *"Polar Wind"*. I could hear the radio on *"Pugster"*, which sounded like a news or current affairs programme, definitely not music.
With the boats being so close together we were all able to converse with each other occasionally without the need to raise our voices.
It was all very idyllic with eight boats, seven from Cromarty Boat Club and one stranger, lying at anchor on a glass-like water surface, broken only by the rings made by the falling rain; it was a nice spot

and was well worth the visit, although I would have preferred to have experienced it in more clement weather. I think if we had gone ashore for the barbecue we would have been eaten alive by the midges.

Turned in early again at around 2000.

Log Reading   4851.8

Total distance covered today 14. 2NM

Tuesday 29th June 2004.

I lay awake for about an hour before getting up at 0730, then made Lilly and myself a cup of tea. I had a quick wash then made some breakfast for myself; Lilly is not a great one for eating first thing in the morning. Whilst I was sitting eating my breakfast, a huge private motor yacht, probably around 100ft long, came into the loch and dropped anchor. This was obviously someone with a lot more money than me, which narrows it down to around 99.9% of the population of the western world.

The arrival of this vessel seemed to have the affect of bringing to life all the other boats in our company and became the talking point for the next twenty minutes.

I began taking down the boom tent and making ready for sea again whilst Lilly got herself washed and dressed. I could see that most of the others were engaged in similar actions.

We left in convoy at 0900 with as usual jock in "*Heart of Gold*" leading the way, he seemed to go closer to the motor yacht than he really required to, some-one made the remark that he was on the lookout for "Totty".

When coming round the point into the Sound o Mull again there was radio traffic with our colleagues in Tobermory, it seemed there was a problem aboard "*Favour*", a hose had been leaking in the engine compartment and had partially flooded the cabin. Although everything was under control they would have to go ashore for the part required.
There was really nothing any of the rest of us could do and they did not expect us to wait for them.

The other two boats, "*Wigeon*" and "*Sun Sieray*" were making preparations to come out and join up with us.
The wind was again more or less against us and with a long day ahead of us I did not relish the idea of beating all the way, so opted instead for motoring although to set the foresail did help a little. Once past the **Eilean Glas** light it was helping us a little bit more as the Sound of Mull takes a little dogleg at that point. Using the engine so much again is eating

into the fuel stocks so I decided to stop off at Loch Aline again to fill up.

As I tied to the jetty I could see that Mike Holmes had followed our course and was five minutes behind me. Gavin informed me that he was intending going right into Loch Aline again, picking up a mooring and having a spot of lunch, he was joined By Mike Wilson and Dave Allan. They appeared in the channel just as I returned to the boat with the petrol.

"*Heart of Gold*" and "*Pugster*", who had both pressed on at a fair speed, must have by that time been somewhere around the Lismore Light.

Both "*Fat Sam*" and "*Wigeon*" now restocked with the *Go-juice* motored back out into the Sound and continued eastwards, "*Kismet*" and "*Norseman*", who had both been doing more sailing than motoring, and had been a good bit behind us, were now almost upon us.

We continued in company to Lismore Light, having discussed, via the radio our plans and our charted course. We were all agreed to the compass course of 080 degrees to take us into Dunstaffanage.

The wind had been rising steadily for the past couple of hours and was now at around a force six and when all four boats had rounded the tip of Lismore Island the foresails were drawing well as the wind was coming from our Starboard quarter. There was quite a swell running and it would make the boat yaw wildly, emptying then filling the foresail and exaggerating the motion of the sea.

I wanted to make the crossing from here as comfortable as possible for Lilly so kept the engine going to cut down on the yawing, it worked quite well and we were managing to maintain a steady speed of six knots with a lot less motion than before, although still somewhat uncomfortable.

Lilly was bearing up quite well, perhaps I was worrying too much about her ability to take the motion and she did admit that she was "not too fond of this" but could suffer it for a while with the thought of a hot shower ahead of us.

On approaching our destination the landscape is so similar that it is difficult to determine the entrance and as I was the lead boat, I radioed Peter, who had been in here before to check that I was indeed heading for the entrance, he confirmed this and in a few minutes we could see all the boats in the marina. I took down the foresail and made ready my warps and fenders.

"*Heart of Gold*" was on the outside pontoon and looked to be the easiest place for me to moor; Jock will be thinking "*Fat Sam*" is his permanent fender!

The facilities at Dunstaffanage are very good with showers, toilets, shops, bar, restaurant and all craning and chandlery services available but like all commercial marinas they are out to take as much money as possible from you.

The overnight charge is £2 per metre, which makes me glad at times like this that I only have a 6 metre boat. On the way to the marina office we saw Jock and Pug in the "Wide mouthed Frog" restaurant, they beckoned us from the window and as soon as we had settled up we joined them for a drink.

Lilly and I ordered a meal, which was very good but a little overpriced at £7.95 for what we had, haddock and chips.

As we were eating I received a call on the mobile from Gavin informing me that he and the remainder of the group were about to enter the channel. It was good to know everyone was here safely. They were quickly situated alongside various pontoons dotted around the Marina and appeared in the bar shortly afterwards.

On finishing the meal we figured it was time for a shower, returning to the boat to collect our toilet gear. When walking back up the pontoons with our towels in hand there was a sudden cloudburst, I was wearing my sailing jacket, which is completely watertight, but it had the effect of directing all the water down onto my unprotected legs soaking them completely.

I made some disparaging remarks about the west coast and the Gaelic translation of the name of this marina meaning "incessant rain", Lilly quickly brought me back down to earth by threatening to get the bus home if I did not stop complaining so vociferously, sometimes think of her like Jiminy Cricket was to Pinocchio, my little conscience!

When I had my shower I felt like a new man and the new man felt like a drink!
Back to the bar for a while but at these prices we did not stop too long and were soon back on board enjoying a G&T with a tin of Guinness (in Lilly's case a vodka & coke).
We retired to bed around 2100.

Log Reading: 4882. 2
Total distance covered today: 30. 4NM

Wednesday 30th June

The morning brought a good wind, which, coming from the southeast was in our favour. There was a lot of radio traffic with Gavin trying to determine who was intending heading for Corpach and who was taking another day to complete the trip. Once it was sorted out into two distinct groups, we agreed a time to set sail and were soon leaving behind the shelter of this bay.

When out in the Lyn of Lorne, the wind was quite brisk but "just what the doctor ordered" as far as direction was concerned and I could reach across the first part to the tip of the point before turning north and running right up past all the little islands that dot this stretch of water.

With the tide also in our favour we managed to make excellent time. Pug, as usual had powered ahead and I watched him as he negotiated "*Pugster*" between the moorings at Port Appin to get alongside the Jetty. He had arranged to meet Robert Hogg here, who was being brought down by Neil & Janice Campbell. At last he would get some sailing done. Gavin and Rod had decided to drop in there too and no doubt there was a fair old "lunch time session" took place at the local hotel.

About a mile ahead of us I could see "*Heart of Gold*" and "*Kismet*" making excellent time and drawing away from us all the time. Peter and Loraine in "*Norseman*" were behind us but they too were sailing very well and were catching up with us. I had my usual shadow in the form of "*Wigeon*" that was sailing with just the jib and a little assistance from the engine. He is still a bit apprehensive on all aspects of sailing, I am sure he will get the hang of it all soon but I do wish he was a bit more adventurous.

Bringing up the rear of this group was "*Pio Moso*".

I passed to the west side of the Isle of Shuna at 1245 and from there the sail up Loch Linnhe was relatively uneventful. The wind had dropped again to little more than a whisper and we had to revert to the motor again.

I had one little incident at Corran Narrows when my engine cut out, Peter stayed on hand until I sorted the problem, an air lock, and we continued on our way.
I need not have worried too much had the engine not re-started as with the strength of the tide at this time, the only place I would have gone was north!

At a rate 4 knots with no power at all I would have shot through the gap like a cork out of a bottle and would not have touched the sides. It is interesting to see the currents here with whirlpools and strange eddies; I would not like to fall in here though as there are very strong undertows.

Norseman waits around to give me assistance

On arrival at Corpach, the leading boats of *"Heart of Gold"* and *"Kismet"* were already inside the lock ready to go up.

Half an hour later all the other boats in our group were Locking up into the basin, where we were then directed to continue up through the next Lock and up into the upper reach as the competitors of the "three peaks race" filled the basin.

A few of us wandered up to the local pub "Trade Winds" and tried to order a meal. "We don't cook on Wednesdays" was the response! What a crock of shit! Bet they complain of a bad season at the end of this year and then blame the Scottish Tourist Board or someone else other than himself or herself for the lack of trade. I won't be back there again and I will make sure everyone I speak to knows of the stupid attitude they have regarding visitor attraction and repeat customers.

What welcome can foreign visitors expect from establishments with "Tunnel Vision" such as those...a little short sighted I would say

Again Lilly and I imposed upon the hospitality of Peter and Loraine and joined them aboard *"Norseman"* for a meal of Pasta and something else; I have forgotten what, as the beer had now started to take its toll.

Lilly said I was "pissed" when I went to bed, but she would say that anyway, might have been true this time though!

Totally oblivious as to what time I went to bed.

Log reading: **4905.3**

Total Distance covered today: 23. 1 NM

Thursday 1ˢᵗ July 2004.

We left the pontoons at 0845 and motored up to the top end of the reach to await the opening of the swing bridge, "*Kismet*" had opted to stay the night at this end and was up and about ready to greet us with a welcoming smile, we tried to get him to make tea for us but when he said no, we had to make our own.

The group of boats had now thinned down to five as "*Wigeon*" was staying until Friday when he would be joined by his wife and brother-in-law to bring the boat up the canal at their leisure.

The swing bridge opened just after nine o'clock allowing all the boats to move forward to the first lock of the Neptune's staircase, where we waited another fifteen minutes before the gates opened. It took over an hour and a half to pass through the flight, as we emerged from the last lock it was approaching 1100.

Once out at the top we continued to motor all the way from Banavie through the Moy swing bridge to Gairlochy locks.

The wind had risen quite considerably and was coming from our stern, which meant that it would be a good "run" up Loch Lochy to Laggan. When in the lock at Gairlochy we got talking to a group of Royal Marine Officers aboard a Naval Sail Training vessel who were bound for Wick.

When "*Fat Sam*" entered the Loch I raised the spinnaker and as soon as it filled, I regretted the decision.

Lilly then started to give me a hard time, I had misjudged the strength of the wind and the boat was yawing wildly from side to side. I asked Lilly to take the helm, until I took the spinnaker down again, but she was not happy at all about this idea.

I took several minutes to convince her that if I did not take it down now it would only get worse and be more difficult to lower later on, reluctantly she helmed whilst I went forward to drop the "Kite".

Even for the short time we had the spinnaker up, about twenty minutes, I had made a lot of ground and was now about a quarter of a mile ahead of any other boat, they were all "goose winging" and I followed their example, using only the working jib. This gave us a steady speed of 6 knots thus helping us to maintain the lead until arriving at Laggan.

The lock gates were closed and we hung about waiting for the next "lock up" by the time this was ready to happen all the other boats were milling around trying to avoid colliding with each other, the wind strength did not help and forced us to keep moving round in circles. Locking in was an experience! The wind was so strong from our stern that I had to have the engine going astern just to slow us down enough not to make contact with any of the other boats. Once the gates closed behind us there was a bit of shelter, this however was short lived as the water rose, lifting the boats and exposing us to the gusts again.

Prior to leaving the Locks at Neptune's Staircase, Lorraine had put together a list of names wishing to have a meal at the "Eagle". Most of the cruisers had opted for this and Lorraine phoned ahead to book us all in. The decision to stay here at Laggan, had therefore been made well in advance.

All the boats were soon alongside the pontoons at the North side of the Lock which would give us an early start the following morning and had the added advantage of affording us a little shelter from the strong winds, ensuring us a reasonably comfortable night's sleep.

We all trooped up to the floating restaurant at 7.30 pm where a seafood platter was set out waiting for us. It included so many species of fish it was difficult note all of them.

Lobster, crab, prawns, salmon to name but a few. This was all topped of with salad and bread and butter. Some chose to order wine with the meal but me being the common 5/8 just plumped for a bottle of stout.

The "Eagle Inn" floating restaurant

Lilly enjoyed it but did not eat a great deal as it is not really what she would normally had gone for, I am sure she would have preferred something simple. The meal cost us £12.50 per head, which was reasonable I suppose but not really being what we wanted I grudged the price a little. All of the others seemed to enjoy it so I held my tongue and did not say what I thought about Hobson's choice.

Once the meal was finished we sat and talked for a while over a couple of drinks but after 9.00 pm everyone started to drift away to their boats and their beds.

Log reading   4917.4

Total distance covered today 12.1 NM

Friday 2nd July 2004

I awoke early and had my shower by 0700 followed by breakfast then stowed the boom tent and made ready for sailing.

0800 we slipped the pontoon and made an uneventful journey to Fort Augustus.
Here again taking the opportunity to replenish the water tank and fuel stocks whilst Lilly went off for some groceries from the local shop.
No sooner had we completed these tasks, the lock gates opened allowing the boats to enter still rafted up together.
There were plenty of hands to take the boats down the flight, as my boat was one of the inside boats my presence was unnecessary so I took the opportunity of sneaking into the Lock Inn for a Guinness.
On leaving the pub I went into the chip shop next door to get some fish and chips. A good number of the other seeing me entering the chip shop yelled out their orders so I became the waiter carrying the food to the workers.

By 1230 the lower Lock gates opened and the boats spilled out into the lower reach and forward to the water of Loch Ness, the wind was very slight and there was barely a ripple on the surface of the Loch, motoring once again!

Somewhere between Foyers and Urquhart Castle a good southerly wind got up allowing us to dispense with the engine, the spinnaker now being the preferred power to take us to the top of Loch Ness.
Gavin called me on my mobile about this time to tell us they were in Loch Oich (a full day behind us) and experiencing torrential rain.

Jock Wingate, in *"Heart of Gold"* was about half an hour ahead of the remainder of us and radioed to ask our position, just as the "Jacobite Queen" passed us in the Dochfour stretch. I relayed this information to him, which he in turn passed on to the Lock keepers. Jock then said that if we could get a move on we would manage to get to the Tomnahurich Bridge for the night, this appealed to me, as there is a pub nearby.
 Although we were cutting it a bit fine to reach the north side of the bridge we managed with minutes to spare, all except *"Pio Moso"* who missed it and had to spend the night on the other side of the main road, still we met them in the pub later.
After a few beers we retuned to the boat at 2100 for a meal of Pasta, turning in not long afterwards for what is our last night on board.

Log Reading.   **4946. 3**

Total distance covered today.   **28. 9 NM**

Saturday 3rd July 2004.

A quick breakfast on rising and moved down to the top of the Muirton Flight at 0800 to await the first flight down, *"Pio Moso"* appeared at 0900 and the gates opened at 0930, two big yachts came out heading south and our little fleet replaced them in the lock.

1015 the swing bridge at the Muirton Basin was swung open giving us access to the basin and the pontoons. From here we would make use of all the facilities, showers, water, fuel and the Co-op shop across the road in Telford Street.
An earlier meeting at the top of the flight had the unanimous agreement to move from the basin at Mid-day. As the hour approached we could all see the dark clouds heading in our direction, this was what Gavin had told me about earlier!
I started to put on my foul weather gear and a quick look round at the other boats indicated that they too were preparing for the worst.

We moved off in convoy through the remaining two locks, stopping at the sea lock to return our keys then out into the Inverness Firth, once again we had salt water beneath our hull. The time now was 1300 and although the tide was still flooding there was not much against us. The wind had dropped a fair bit but the rain had started to fall quite heavily. I set a foresail and kept the engine running to aid our progress.

I set a course across the Skate Bank and passed under the centre span off the Kessock Bridge. By the time Chanonry point was on the beam, the tide had started to ebb and would give us valuable assistance on the run to Cromarty. At this point the rain was coming down harder than I had ever experienced, so much that the self-draining cockpit in "*Fat Sam*" was straining to cope with the amount of water falling and the cockpit was permanently half full. Visibility was down to almost Zero and I lost sight of "*Kismet*" and "*Heart of Gold*" who were both less than fifty yards behind me. Jock and I are familiar with the waters around this area so neither of us was unduly concerned but I learned from Andy Young later that he was desperate to keep one or both of us in his sights to act as a guide.

The rain continued its relentless downpour for the rest of the journey to Cromarty Firth; steering solely by compass, it was far too wet to bring the GPS out of the cabin, I would get an occasional quick glimpse of the "Byford Dolphin" Oil Rig that would confirm my position.

As "*Fat Sam*" entered the Cromarty Firth, with the Buss Bank Buoy fifty yards to starboard, the rain had eased very slightly and I could see, "*Ben Crom*", the dredger working in and out of the harbour.

I called him on Channel 16, was instructed to go to channel 6, I informed him that there were four club boats on the way in and would like to have a clear entrance to the harbour. He said he would give us plenty room but warned us that the tide was ebbing at 6 knots through the harbour mouth.

Entering the harbour was "interesting", but we managed without any incident, I was followed closely by Jock then Andy appeared and had a little more difficulty than we did but came to no harm. Peter and Lorraine opted to pass the harbour and head straight for their mooring; in the meantime I headed for the pub with Lilly. The time was now 1600.

I decided to leave the boat in the harbour overnight and empty all the cruising gear in the morning. Everyone was tired and wet but we had a couple of beers and celebrated the completion of another successful Cromarty Boat Club Cruise.

Log reading.   4961. 0

Total distance covered today.   14. 7 NM

Total Distance covered during the whole two weeks   206. 6 NM

Heart Problems

The end of the **2004** season brought new problems to me. Although now over 60 I still tried to keep reasonably fit and used to run a mile every morning before breakfast. This had been becoming more and more difficult and I always felt so tired. I put it down to getting older and thought that I would just have to accept this.

When running one morning I thought I had heartburn and kept wishing it would go away.

It was not until I felt the pain down my left arm that I realised it was not heartburn.

After a short stay in hospital, I was informed there was nothing wrong with my heart.

I returned to work only to collapse in the road one day and was rushed to hospital.

I spent the next month in and out of Raigmore and Aberdeen Royal Infirmary where I was fitted with a stent and life came back to normal.

The cruise in **2005** was a very downbeat affair where we had a leisurely sail along the Moray coast calling at Lossiemouth, Buckie, and Whitehills then back to Findhorn and home. I am sure I had a log of this trip but I am unable to find it.

Some of the boats in Buckie harbour 2005

Full Orkney Cruise

2006: Following the success of the "Orkney or Bust" cruise in 2003, I still had Orkney in my system and would not be happy until I had completed a cruise which would circumnavigate the islands calling at several places I had only read about.
I wanted to see them for myself aboard my own boat "*Fat Sam*".

During the "Commodores Cruise" skippers meeting, held in January 2006, I intimated that I would like to cruise to Orkney once again, only this time making it over a two-week period so as to allow time to visit some of the other islands.

After a discussion, agreement was reached that we would sail from Cromarty on Saturday 1st July with the intention of calling at *Helmsdale, Wick, St Margaret's Hope, Stromness, Pierowall on Westray, Whitehall on Stronsay, Kirkwall, Lamb Holm, Wick and return to Cromarty.*

I then enlisted a local man, "Ginga" MacPhee, to crew me for the trip, he was a bit unsure at first, saying he knew nothing about sailing a yacht.

I assured him I had more than enough knowledge for both of us and I only needed someone for company and for opening cans of beer. At the mention of beer, he accepted.

The passage plan was then prepared and made allowances for a few days off during the trip and a few more days built in for flexibility. As is often the case in sailing, prevailing circumstances dictate a change to the original plan, normally because of the weather, this trip was no different, and we had to make changes to our plan by the time we reached Pierowall.

This is an account of the trip.

Saturday 1ˢᵗ July 2006
Time 0710, Log Reading: 5696.5

As always seems to happen when Cromarty Boat Club set off on a cruise the forecast is for little or no wind for the first two days.
Ever the optimists, however, six boats set sail from Cromarty on a flat calm morning, they were:
"Kismet": with Andy Young, sailing single-handed from here to Wick
"Norseman": Peter Baxter and Lorraine Beigley aboard.
"Evening Light": Owned and skippered by Gwyn Phillips, his crew was Ron King.
"Tunnag": This had the inseparable pair of Bill Paterson and his crewmember Alex Davidson.
"Marion": His wife Wilma accompanied Archie Murray
"Fat Sam": With my Crew of Ginga and myself as Skipper.

All the Boats left in line like a wartime convoy of RN Ships (this remark will upset the ex Merchant men in the group!)
By the time we reached the Sutors under power there was a very slight breeze but not enough to give us any great headway. I had to content myself with the engine. This seemed ok by Ginga as he needed some time to familiarise himself with the strange surroundings of a yacht. He asked a multitude of questions about the standing rigging,

the running rigging, the sails, the keel and all other things that were obviously alien to a man who had spent most of his life at sea on fishing boats.

I have to admit though, that every question was a genuine and intelligent demand for the proper information.

He would watch me closely as I took compass bearings for fixes and observe me as I noted them on the chart, then cross check using the GPS. It would appear I have stirred an interest in him for navigation.

By the time we reached Tarbet Ness a slight wind had come up from the East and the sails at last showed signs of filling. We managed to hold the wind for a good time but it was backing all the time. Around two miles out from Helmsdale, it was coming straight from the North.

This is another regular occurrence, if there is any wind at all for us on our annual cruise; it is normally on the nose!

I decided it was time for the motor again, as we were getting hungry and we would have to stock up our petrol supplies and have everything ship shape before heading off to the pub to watch the football on the telly.

We made our way up to the local filling station with the petrol cans, returning ten minutes later to stow them aboard. Ginga treated me to a meal of fish and chips as a thank you for inviting him along on the cruise; he was beginning to enjoy himself.

After the football game finished we had one more pint then returned to the boat, I worked on the next days passage info as Ginga again watched me, taking it all in, I then decided to go to my bed ready for the early start in the morning, my crew followed suit.

By 2130 I was tucked up in my bed, a voice form the forward cabin said: *"half past nine at night and I'm in my bed! I haven't done this since I was in Porterfield!"*
(Porterfield is HMP in Inverness)

Log reading 5723.0

Distance today 26.5NM

Accumulative Mileage: 26.5NM

Sunday 2nd July 2006

The toilet and shower facilities at Helmsdale are a vast improvement to the days when we had to walk 500yds to the nearest public toilet, which was usually closed at night.
By 0600 all the skippers and crews were showered and fed and ready to sail.

Archie then informed the rest of the fleet that with Wilma feeling unwell he was reluctantly returning to

Cromarty, although Wilma was feeling poorly, she was also a little upset that she was depriving Archie of further participation on the cruise.

The first boat left the harbour mouth at 0630 and headed north again followed in close succession by the other four. We could see the solitary outline of "*Marion*" as it headed in the general direction of home, gradually disappearing over the horizon.

Shortly after leaving Helmsdale there was a huge splash off to our starboard, I was looking in the direction as it happened and could clearly see that it was a Minke Whale, Ginga had heard it but did not see the animal.

Having learned that it was a Minke he spent the next few hours eagerly waiting for a repeat showing, which unfortunately for him never materialised.

Wind was again today very light and although I raised the mainsail for the trip we again had to motor for the first four hours.
An audio conference was held via the VHF radio and a collective decision is made to stop for a couple of hours in Lybster for brunch, "*Fat Sam*" arriving at 1030 some of the skippers and crews headed up the steep hill toward the town for a walk or to get a daily paper. I chose to stay on board and have something to eat.

1215 and time to set sail again, although I say "set sail" it is in fact to motor, as there is still not enough wind to take us, it would have been cheaper to drive up than to come by boat!

Around 1500, Wick is now in sight, I remark that we have sailed all day and never again did we set eyes on a Minke, Ginga replied *"we will see plenty in Wick and they are all related to me!"*

On approaching Wick harbour at 1545, the harbourmaster gave us directions over the VHF to moor close to the fish market in the outer harbour, this suits us fine, as we are closer to the shower block here. There are already a number of boats alongside the wall and closer inspection tells us they are from Nairn Sailing Club, they too are on an Orkney cruise calling at similar ports to us but in an anti-clockwise direction rather than the clockwise direction as chosen by us.

Three big charter boats of over 40ft join us soon after, returning from an Orkney cruise, heading for to their homeport of Largs via the Caledonian Canal.

A bunch of us head into town to the Wetherspoons Restaurant for a meal, there is an offer of two meals for the price of one, which includes fish and chips; I convince Ginga that this is what we should have. Each of the boats remains in their own groups when buying the meal and any drinks.

A couple of hours later we return to the boats via Camps bar, Ginga finds a kindred spirit in the barman who was also a fisherman and they reminisced over fishing boats that are long since broken up or lost at sea (a truly cheerful subject to discuss when on a sailing holiday!).

Once back down at the harbour we have an impromptu party aboard evening light with music supplied by Gwyn on Guitar, with me doing most of the singing.

The sound of this soon attracts the guys from most of the other boats, who bring with them their own musical instruments that lead to a very enjoyable evening's entertainment, at one point there were over thirty people in the party.

Ginga had once told me that he played the guitar very badly and as if to prove this point, borrowed Gwyn's, he was allowed the use of this for at least two minutes!

I retired at midnight

Log Reading: 5753.1

Distance today 30.1 NM
Accumulative Mileage: 56.6NM

Monday 3rd July 2006

1230, Neil Campbell, who was joining Bill and Alex as far as Stromness, arrived with Ken Muir who was to be Andy Young's crew for the remainder of the trip.

I had calculated the time to leave Wick in order to have the most favourable tidal conditions in the Pentland Firth would be 1500, arriving at Duncansby Head at around 1830, one hour and twenty minutes before High Water Aberdeen.

I had reached this conclusion by studying the passage information and the Tidal Atlas for the area. There were differing opinions from the other boats regarding the time, which led to lengthy discussions on the matter. The contradictory plans of each boat had come about because we were working on different Tidal information, I was using Aberdeen some were using Dover and others Ullapool or Wick times. They should still come out at roughly the same though!

A compromise was reached and reluctantly I set sail with the fleet at 1330, although I am still not happy with the situation, as we will arrive well over an hour before my initial estimated time.
To attempt to cross the Pentland Firth at the wrong time is folly, this is the most dangerous stretch of water in the whole of Europe!

During the passage from Wick up to Duncansby Head I slowed right down to waste some more time, Ginga asked if it was all that important, I replied that it could mean the difference between living and dying! That seem to focus his mind somewhat and he remained quiet for a while.

He asked if I wanted a beer, my reply of *"I'd rather wait until the Pentland Firth is behind us"* had the effect of silencing him again. *"Evening Light"* motored alongside us and called to me *"We are going to be too early"* I told him that is why I had slowed down to a crawl. Gwyn and I have sailed several cruises together and our calculations are never very far apart, I would always double check my figures if they showed a great variance to his. We have a mutual respect for each other's ability in Navigational Skills. He too then slowed down to the same speed as *"Fat Sam"*.

On seeing this, all of the others had now adopted the same tactic
Looking round I could see that all the others had now dropped speed quite considerably and I was in fact now passing them.
By the time we did reach the waypoint I was the leading boat and even adopting such a slow pace for such a length of time, I reckoned we were still almost an hour too early
The wind was non existent as we passed *Duncansby Head*, as it is the wind over tide that creates most of the problems in this stretch of water I decided to proceed and radioed my intentions to the remainder now in my wake. I told them to watch me closely and to listen out for my radio transmission should there be a problem I would let them know.

This was to the delight of Ginga who proclaims that it is *"like sailing with Geronimo, who always leads the way!"*

To begin with we were stemming the tide but as we arrived abeam of the island of Swona, the GPS indicated that we had in fact picked up the North going tide; I relayed the information to all the boats some of which were now over two miles behind us.

With the tide now in our favour we made excellent progress and by 1930, *"Fat Sam"* was leaving *Pentland Firth* behind and rounding *Hoxa Head* into *Scapa Flow.*

I asked Ginga if he would now pour me a glass of Guinness, this was somewhat of a relief to him and he gladly obliged.

Within 45 minutes I had dropped anchor in the quiet little bay at *St Margaret's Hope.* I quickly inflated the rubber dinghy and was ashore fifteen minutes later, two minutes to the Murray Arms, order a quick pint of Guinness and ask about meals.

We were now informed that meals stop being served at 2030; I explained that there are five boats with a minimum of two aboard that are in need of food. The bar staff agreed to go through to speak to the cook, who appeared a minute later, I said "hello Barbara" thankfully she recognised me from the last trip here and she agreed to keep the kitchen open to feed us, providing we took something simple like fish and chips. We agreed and I returned to the shore to relay the message to the others, who by now, were all at anchor, I confirmed numbers requiring a meal, "*Kismet*" and "*Norseman*" chose to stay on board,) and I returned to tell Barbara of the numbers.

Twenty minutes later a happy group of sailors were eating fish and chips whilst washing it down with copious amounts of beer, happiness is bliss!

After a while, with the conversation about the Pentland Firth exhausted, we decide it is time to call it a day and made our way back to the boats to prepare for the day ahead tomorrow.

Another successful crossing of the dreaded Pentland Firth is behind us

Log Reading: 5783.4

Distance today 30.3 NM
Accumulative Mileage: 86.9NM

Tuesday 4Th July 2006

I awoke at 0700, rose and washed, soon followed by Ginga and we breakfasted before weighing anchor an rafting up alongside starboard side of "*Tunnag*", with "*Evening Light*", rafted up to his port side. Today's intended sail is a relatively simple and short sail of around 12 NM across the Scapa Flow, we compared our sail plans, nothing contentious, a quick call to the other two boats and we were on our way at 0830.

Ginga had shown he was capable of sailing the boat well now and I gave him the tiller for most of the way across Scapa Flow.

I could then concentrate on the Navigation and act as *His* crew during the passage.

This was an excellent arrangement and he relished the idea that he was now in charge whilst under sail.

We were "Goose winging" (this is a way of sailing with the wind dead astern, with the Main out to one side and the Foresail to the other catching as much wind as possible) all the way across the Flow with a favourable South-easterly breeze, at one point we were being overtaken by *"Kismet"*, when the wind gave a slight shift. I went forward to gybe the foresail and was coming aft to carry out the same manoeuvre with the Mainsail.

Ginga had seen me doing several tasks at the same time whilst sailing and assumed it was easy enough to handle the main sheet and the tiller at the same time. He decided that if it was good enough for me, then it is good enough for him.... Wrong!!

With his mind focused on changing the sail over to the other side he left the tiller alone and failed to keep the boat under control and/or sailing in a straight line, the boat lurched to Starboard and was heading for *"Kismet"*; we were about to punch a hole in the port quarter of Andy's pride and joy!

Full marks to Ginga; he grabbed the Tiller again and threw the boat *hard* to starboard, missing the stern of the other boat by several inches.

Note:
1. Never again during the cruise did Ginga try multitasking.
2. Whenever we were in the vicinity of "*Kismet*", Andy would check who was at the helm!

We arrived in Stromness just after midday, just as we approached the marina the roller reefing jammed and I was unable to pull the foresail in, I went forward to clear it, leaving Ginga in charge: with the explicit instructions to keep away from other boats!
We tied up on the new pontoons, which were not there on our previous visit, and Steve, the marina supervisor introduced himself and said he would return at 1815 for the dues.

We all then made our way up to the Ferry Inn for a meal; I had fish and chips again! I later returned to the boat to pay the dues leaving Ginga making a valiant attempt to drink the bar dry.
I paid the dues and Steve passed over very useful info on the facilities for here and other Marinas in the Orkneys.
I lay down for a while on my bunk to read but fell into a deep sleep, I am sure I would have slept right through to the morning had it not been for a voice penetrating my sleep:
"*Fat Sam, Fat Sam, this is Ginga. Over*". The call was repeated several times before I was fully awake to realise it was coming from the roadway above the Marina and not the Radio as I first thought.

I looked out to see Ginga, barely able to bite his fingernails. He had locked himself out of the Marina and could not use the combination code to access entry.

I had to get up and walk about 250 yards to let him in.

I would have to get used to this, situations like this were to become a regular occurrence for the remainder of the cruise.

Log Reading: 5796.3

Distance today 12.9NM

Accumulative Mileage: 99. 8 NM

Wednesday 5th July 2006

Rest Day:

We had discussed at length the idea of moving on today and taking the scheduled "Rest Day" further on. The weather forecast made up our minds for us and we stayed put.

Everyone decided what he or she wanted to do and split into several groups' activities.

Peter, Lorraine and Andy hired a car to visit *Skara Brae*, Ken and Ron went off to visit an old friend,

Gwyn, Alex, Bill and I visited the Stromness museum and Ginga went, you've guessed it, to the pub.

Fed up with the smell of smoke on the boat I decided to try and stop Ginga from smoking aboard. In the town I found a sticker for no smoking and went back to the boat to fix it in the cockpit.
Later on in the afternoon we met up with him in the "Flattie" Bar of the Stromness Hotel.
After a few pints I tried to persuade him to come back to the boat with me but to no avail.

At 1830 Andy Young appeared at my boat asking for the key to the shower block, which of course, Ginga had in his pocket!
Again I went up the town to find him, there are only three places he could have been, I found him in the third, The Royal Hotel bar.

I got the key and again tried to convince him that coming back to the boat was the best idea, he was having none of it.
After I left him he must have had second thoughts for he returned to the boat around half an hour behind me. I was having a meal when he stepped on board and seeing me eating said, *"Do you have any other hobbies apart from eating?"*

At 2000 he lay down on his bunk for a short kip, intending to go back out later to "top up" the alcohol levels. He fell into a deep sleep, I did not wish to disturb him so let him sleep on; he slept right through to the following morning.

I now had peace and quiet, apart from the rumble of his snoring, to prepare the passage plan for tomorrow.

I took to my bed just after 2100.

Thursday 6th July 2006

There was much activity with all the boat crews coming and going to the showers and the usual breakfast organising.   Ginga went out into the cockpit and lit up his morning "smoke" I said, *"Did you see this?"*

Pointing to my new sticker

Ginga carried on drawing on his "roll up" and as he breathed out a lung full of smoke said, *"If I see any Puffins on board I will kick them off!"*

0900 we slipped our moorings for what was to be one of the longest legs, out into the Atlantic Ocean and round the Orkney Mainland to come into the Westray firth and up into Pierowall.

As we motored out through Hoy Mouth, the "*Wind over Tide*" was causing serious overfalls that "*Norseman*" seemed hell bent on going through. Closer inshore there were waves breaking over rocks.

Ginga was feeling rather fragile after his boozing binge the previous day and the sight of "*Norseman*" being tossed about like a cork on the port bow and huge breakers on the starboard bow made him feel even worse.

He asked what was causing the turbulence being experienced by Peter and Lorraine; I explained it was tide wanting to go one way and the wind trying to force the water another way. He then asked, "*Is that rocks in there?*" when I said yes he asked, "*Where the hell are we going?*" I replied "*in that little narrow strip between the two dangers.* "

"*Fat Sam*", "*Tunnag*", "*Evening Light*" and "*Kismet*", all negotiated the narrow strip of quiet water between the two disturbances. Ginga had gone deathly quiet again until we were clear of the hazards.

The wind at this moment in time was blowing 4-5 south-easterly and we had a great sail up past *Marwick Head*, where *HMS Hampshire* was sunk in 1916 with the loss of life of 643 sailors including Lord Kitchener and his staff.

We could clearly see the Kitchener memorial high up on the cliff top as we sailed past.

When we passed *Brough head* at the NW tip of the Orkney mainland the wind veered and decreased in strength, from here until we were passing *Sacquoy head*, on the *Island of Rousay*, the wind was variable and at times we had to motor to keep our scheduled waypoints on time.

This part of the leg was very interesting as we were experiencing some of the big Atlantic swells and boats 100 yards away from us would disappear beneath the swell with only the top of their mast visible above the crest of the water.

Ginga and I discussed every possible subject during this long leg and I found him to be very knowledgeable on an array of different subjects, this had the result of making the long day seem shorter.

As we entered the *Westray Firth* the wind started to pick up again and allowed us to continue sailing up through *Rapness Sound* and *Weatherness Sound*, when I rounded into *North Sound*, I was able to raise the spinnaker and gain some ground on the boats that had managed to overhaul us. Ahead off us was *Skelwick Skerry*, with all the boats taking this to port I decided to check the chart and realising I had enough depth I took it to starboard.

This pleased Ginga no end and again was shouting *"Geronimo"!*

As it turned out we were the second boat to enter *Pierowall Roads*, "Evening Light", under power from his "Iron Spinnaker" was two cables ahead of us and was tied up in the harbour by the time we entered between the pier ends.

The time was now 1745; it had taken us under nine hours to complete the trip which meant we achieved an average of 4 knots which is exactly what I had allowed for.

We had all heard that the fish and chips at the local hotel were the best in the world and went off as a group to find out.

The hotel is a decent stretch of the legs from the harbour being over a mile away but the banter between all the crews going and returning was worth the walk. Gavin Meldrum phoned me from his boat on the west coast to get an update on our progress I gladly obliged telling where we were and details of the trip so far.

I joined Andy and some of the others aboard his Hunter Horizon 26 for a quick drink and a chat about what we have achieved so far and what tomorrow holds in store for us. I returned to my own boat at around 2200 but not before spilling a glass of red wine over Andy's upholstery (sorry once again Andy!)

Log Reading: 5831.8

Distance today 35.5NM

Accumulative Mileage: 135.3NM

Friday 7th July 2006

Ginga was up and off for a shower at 0530, his understanding from the night before was that we were due to leave at 0700.

The wind was very strong at that moment, 4-5 gusting 6 from the SW. We were hoping to leave at 1330 but the weather did not look very promising and the forecast was for the wind to continue.

Ginga went to the local fish processing plant and came back with fresh crab; he then went below and using up the rest of the vegetable salad, before it went off, produced a very tasty crab salad for our lunch.

The forecast for the following few days was not good at all and the fleet had decided to make straight for Kirkwall as soon as possible, an update for today's forecast was for the wind to decrease slightly in the afternoon and by 1400 it had eased off a little. A quick word with the harbour master confirmed that the tide would still be in our favour (local knowledge is always handy to have!) for the trip to Kirkwall. We made a collective decision to go for the small weather window we had.

One small problem was that the boats were being pushed against the pontoon with the way the wind was, again the harbour master came to our assistance and took a line from the other side of the harbour to pull the head of each boat in turn away from the pontoon until they had enough power on to clear the harbour.

"Fat Sam" was first boat out of Pierowall and we led the way down *Pierowall Roads* and out into *North Sound*, then followed the reciprocal course from yesterday until we reached *Weather Ness* and instead of going south through *Rapness Sound* we had chosen the alternative passage through the *Sound of Faray*, this Sound has little or no tidal flow. As we crossed into the top end of the sound the tide was setting across our bows from West to East but the effect was short lived and the remainder of the sail down to *Westray Firth*, about, three and a half miles, was calm and very enjoyable.

When we sailed out into the *Westray Firth* I radioed the other boats to remind them that the tide was setting in a direction of 150 degrees at a rate of 2 knots.

I set a course for the south Cardinal Mark at the tip of the island of *Egilsay*, the bearing was 210 degrees but with the tide and leeway taken into consideration I steered a course of 245 degrees, this proved to be the perfect course as we arrived at the cardinal mark at my planned ETA. From this point to the next waypoint the tide was not quite as severe and the remainder of this leg, down past *Girsay* and onto *Kirkwall* was fairly straightforward.

We made radio contact with Kirkwall harbour and were directed to keep the Coastguard Cutter to starboard, turn to port on entering the harbour and take up any of the vacant pontoon berths ahead of us.

I was tied up alongside by 2000, closely followed by the others; within thirty minutes we were all secured.

With the weather reports we had been receiving it looked as though we would probably be here for several days.

Couple of beers at the local pub and a shower at the yacht club, but nothing spectacular happened that night.

Log Reading: 5853.1
Distance today 21.3 NM
Accumulative Mileage: 156.6NM

Saturday 8th July 2006

I was awakened very early in the morning with the arrival of several boats, as I was near the end of the pontoon, any boat causing a bow wave would make our boat roll slightly and this wakened me.

It was the finish of the "Orkney Challenge Race" from Lossiemouth and there was a steady stream of arrivals between 0500 and 0800.

As we walked up to the pub during the day I saw a boat with the Home Port of "*Gosport*" I got talking to him and learned that he is living aboard his Hunter designed *Mystery* 35, *"Aragorn"* Robert Jollye was to become part of our group over the coming week and would end up joining the Cromarty Boat Club.

The rest of the day was spent just pottering around but we did end up in the Kirkwall Yacht Club at night for the presentation of the prizes for the Orkney Challenge.

Our happy little band supplied the music during the event but as usual the "Lossiemouth Crowd" would not mix with us. It sad that some clubs still try to make out that they are an elite group and find it difficult to interact with other clubs, this in my view is what is the matter with our chosen sport, there are so many pretentious people who portray the whole sport as an elitist pastime.

However there is a lighter side to this, Ginga arrived and managed to bring the whole proceedings down to basics, he pulled out a stool, sat down, missing the stool and sadly ended up on his backside on the deck. He did several other "party tricks" during the night but I will save him the embarrassment of repeating them all.

Sunday 9th July 2006

I woke up to find that the strong winds that had been forecast had not yet materialised.
After showering and a good breakfast we spent most of the day wandering around *Kirkwall*. Visited *St Magnus Cathedral*, had a few more beers before returning to the boat for a bite to eat. We all then went back up to watch the world cup football on the television in the pub. Ginga had spent most of, or all

of the day in the Queens, with the occasional visit to the bookies so when we arrived back at the pub he was a little the worse for wear and decided to return to the boat on his own.

We watched the Football and afterwards went back to the boats. As soon as I stepped aboard "Fat Sam", it woke Ginga who, now having had a sleep, was ready for hitting the town again and off he went.

Cromarty Boat Club boats in Kirkwall

I had a couple of hours chatting with the other guys before retiring.

At around 2.00am I was awakened by the sound a voice shouting *"May Day, May Day, Distress, Fat Sam, this is Ginga"* I sat up in bed and looked round to see his bunk empty, I shouted, *"Where the hell are you?"*
"I'm in the water" was the reply.

I quickly jumped up and was out on deck, then onto the pontoon within seconds, I spotted him immediately hanging onto the edge of the pontoon walkway board.
I knew I would be unable to lift him out by myself so jumped back on board to get a line to secure him before going for assistance; however, Peter and Lorraine had also heard the commotion and were now running towards us.
Peter and I each managed to get an arm under his armpits and lifted him clear of the water, Lorraine then grabbed his lower legs and between us we got him onto his feet on the staging.
He was shivering uncontrollably with the cold and was probably in the early stages of hypothermia.

As he leaned against the guardrail of the boat, I was trying to get him on board and into a dry sleeping bag as soon as possible. He on the other hand, had the idea of engaging in conversation in some foreign language unknown to me.
I was very concerned for his condition and the only way I could impress upon him the importance of getting on board and into his bunk, was to give him

several sharp punches to the ribs, he eventually got the idea and in due course was in his bunk.

I lay awake for ages listening to him shivering and breathing erratically, at one point I was going to phone for an ambulance but he drifted off to sleep and his breathing became near normal. I continued to listen out for a while but he seemed to settle quite well and I in turn slipped into unconsciousness.

Monday 10th July 2006

The arrival of the morning saw a very subdued Ginga; I think that last nights close encounter with his maker had now dawned on him. I also thought that there may have been a little bit embarrassment involved too.
He made an endeavour to thank me for saving his life but I tried to play it down by saying that in similar circumstances I would like to think he would do the same for me, I felt there was no need to humiliate him any further.

The wind was a little stronger than had been of late but with still no sign of the gales that were forecast. I met up with Peter and Gwyn during the morning to see if it was worth while gaining access to internet facilities to get a better picture of what weather patterns were in fact having influences over us.

We found that the library in Kirkwall allows free Internet access and made our way there just before lunchtime, this reiterated what the Coastguard stations had already told us, that severe weather was still in fact imminent. We just have to wait and see what happens!

Every cloud has a silver lining; we found a Lidl Supermarket and decided to stock up on our depleting essential stocks, gin, tonic and Guinness! I also bought a very useful sailing bag for £7.99, this is completely waterproof and designed like a kit bag, and it proves to be the very thing!

As per usual we called into the pub on the way back to the boat; Ginga was there but was sober and still very quiet.
After I returned to the boat in the afternoon, Ginga appeared shortly after me and handed me an envelope with £100 voucher for meals at the Queens Hotel, this was by way of appreciation to me, Peter and Lorraine for our assistance the previous night.
I took the envelope and found Peter and Lorraine to tell them that I thought this was a bit "over the top", they both agreed but pointed out that if we did not accept something it would make him feel bad.

All three of us met up at the Queens for the said meal at 1830, we had a quick word with the management and explained the situation asking if we could buy just a simple meal and have the unused value returned in cash, this was agreed.

We spent about £20 between us, and returned £80 in cash to Ginga thanking him for the gesture. Let no more be said on the matter!

We had a few quiet beers again before retiring, I did however, make sure my crewmember came with me.

Tuesday 11th July 2006

The wind was here at last, not that I wanted it! Today it was blowing at least an eight, we were thankful not to be out there in it.

I just wish it would pass over us and let us get on with our sailing!

There is only so much one can find to do in Kirkwall. Today it was laundry, and yes the Pub!

Gwyn and Ron have decided to get the ferry home rather than sit it out here. Gwyn has lots of things he can be doing with his business. They left by bus at 0900 to catch the ferry at Burry across to John O'Groats. Gwyn phoned me from the ferry to tell me that the waves were breaking over the bows and spilling water right down both sides; just as well we were tucked up safely in the harbour here.

I was so fed up with the situation that I had recorded virtually nothing in the log for today, just another boring day in this otherwise lovely city.

Wednesday 12th July 2006.

The wind was still with us, not a lot more to do and see here, library, supermarkets and back to the pub. Getting a little bit of harbour rot now!

Thursday 13th July 2006

Wind was still very strong but was showing signs of abating, thank God!

I spent a lot of time working on my passage plan for tomorrow in the hope that we can get away first thing in the morning. We did go up for a pub lunch but we were back on board fairly early to have a skippers meeting and compare notes of the intended passage.

There was a slight difference of opinion again; on this occasion regarding the time we should be entering the *String*. (This is the stretch of water between the Orkney Mainland and the Isle of Shapinsay) where the tide is very strong, getting the time wrong can mean going at several knots in the wrong direction.

My calculations prefer 0800 start to arrive at the string 30 minutes later, Peter on the other hand wants to leave an hour earlier, compromise time again and we eventually agree to depart as a convoy at 0740.

Friday 14th July 2006

By the time we got ready and slipped our lines we were leaving the harbour in convoy at 0750, which was only ten minutes ahead of my original calculation, the tide was still slightly against us but in this part of the world changes from flood to ebb with little or no slack water time. The wind was a little fickle at first and we spent short periods of sail then motoring until we reached *Carr Ness* at 0820, which is the next waypoint at the entrance to the String, so we are not far off what I wanted.

The next two hours would see us through the *Sound of Shapinsay* and out into *North Sea* just off *Mull Head*. The chart shows that there are severe overfalls here, but the wind was not very strong at the time and I decided to sail close in to take advantage of the tidal stream and at one point registered 10 knots over the ground when my log tells me we were doing 4, a six knot tide is a great help!

The other boats had sailed well clear of the *Mull Head* and I had overtaken all but one (*Kismet*) by the time we were half way down to the *Horse of Copinsay*, an isolated rock just North of the *Isle of Copinsay*.

Ginga spent most of the day inquiring where are we, how do you know that's what you are looking at, what are tidal diamonds, how do you work out the

209

course and a host of other equally searching questions. I continue to supply answers and he continues to ask questions. I think I have at last found the ideal student for my winter navigation courses, his interest is fantastic!

The Island of Copinsay

Wick was still a long way off but during my studying of the chart for the passage showed that we could actually carry the tide for NINE hours if we sailed the proper course.

I set the course for passing the *Pentland Skerries* five miles to starboard, at one point, the tidal stream was much stronger than predicted and I find we were being pulled toward the Skerries and I started the motor to assist in getting back to the course I want.

All around the boat the water was disturbed by the phenomenal tides in this area with so many whirlpools and rips it is difficult to describe accurately. Looking westward to the Skerries it seems as though there is a "wall" of water, an odd sight indeed!

We were still carrying the tide at 1700 although it was almost spent, in another twenty minutes it would be against us, we were now South East of *Duncansby head* and I could see *Noss Head* on our Starboard Bow, about 6 miles off. We continued to sail for around another 30 minutes but I finally made the decision to motor sail the remaining few miles as we were getting tired now.

Wick was a welcoming sight and as we made our approach "*Aragorn*" managed to catch up with the Cromarty boats and we entered the Harbour almost together at 1845.

We spent a little time exchanging anecdotes about the journey down before making our way up to Wetherspoons restaurant, where we commandeered three tables to accommodate all the crews and had a communal meal.

When we got back to the boats, tomorrows passage plan was prepared (It will be good to sail again in very familiar waters) we all agreed that we would make an early start then had a couple of beers.

I turned in early and left the rest of the crews sitting around talking, I lay in my bunk listening to the banter and as I lay there I looked up to see a couple standing staring down at me from the dockside. From their position they could see right into the boat and were looking directly at me.

I shouted up to them, "*Could I have your address so that I can come round and stare into your bedroom*"? They then left!

Log Reading: 5895.5
Distance today 42.4 NM

Accumulative Mileage: 199.0NM

Saturday 15th July 2006

As agreed the night before we were all up at the crack of dawn for a shower and breakfast before heading out into the Moray Firth. Bill Paterson in the lead boat passed the breakwater light at 0600 followed again in convoy by the rest of us.

I was not really looking forward to the long sail ahead as it would probably take us in excess of twelve hours to get to Cromarty.

There was a very good wind again for most of the day, with periods when it dropped away completely and we spent a lot of time under power, the good thing about this, is that I put the auto helm on and let the boat take us home on its own for parts of the day whilst Ginga and I talked about every subject imaginable.

Several times we did manage to get the sails filled but each time it was short lived for perhaps an hour or more then we went back to motoring for a while then the wind returned again and remained steady for the remainder of the leg home.

It was a pretty uneventful journey back to Cromarty; this always seems to be the case on the return leg of any cruise. It's a bit of an anti climax sailing home after an adventure.

The navigation was relatively simple as I know these waters very well and can recognise all the headlands and navigation points without having to consult charts and almanacs.

After what seemed to be an eternity we were at last in sight of the Sutors and although we were sailing at quite a leisurely pace, we should be inside the Cromarty firth by 1830.

"Fat Sam" passed the Buss bank buoy around 1815 and we were safely inside Cromarty Harbour by 1900. We all adjourned to the pub for a quick one before removing some of our gear then securing the boat for the night.

I would empty the majority of my gear in the morning at my leisure, another cruise ends and I strolled up the road the house to see my ever patient wife Lilly and of course my Golden Labrador Corrie, both of whom are delighted to see me (no accounting for taste then!!)

Log Reading 5951.9
Distance Today 56.4NM

Accumulative Mileage 255.4

I had a great time with Ginga on this his first cruise and the words of the song are an accurate record of his exploits

Ginga MacPhee

To the Tune "The Mountains of Mourne"

Come closer and listen, I'll tell you a tale
Of a Cromarty man who crewed me on a sail
He had served aboard Trawlers and Drifters a lot
But never before had he been on a Yacht
I could tell by his manner that he had been around
He was quick in his wit and his judgement was sound
But I never imagined the things I would see
When I press-ganged my crewmember Ginga MacPhee

The morning we sailed out, there was a fresh breeze
With the boat heeling over, he seemed ill at ease
I could see he was worried by the look in his eyes
But I quickly assured him we would not capsize
I tried to convince him we were not going to sink
And suggested he might feel at ease with a drink
So he poured out a large one and another for me
My very good crewmember Ginga MacPhee

He asked lots of questions right from the start
And had a thirst for the knowledge I had to impart
He listened intently as he took it all in
While drinking my stocks of both Guinness and Gin
But two days hard training it sure did the trick
He could sail very well by the time we reached Wick
If he keeps up at this rate he'll be better than me
My quick learning crewmember Ginga MacPhee

But speaking quite bluntly, a problem he's got
When he gets too much drink he just loses the plot
One night moored in Stromness, as I lay in my bed
The sound of his voice penetrated my head
I opened the hatches and I saw this Buffoon
So full of drink, could not reach the pontoon
I know no one else who can drink quite like he
My booze-loving crewmember Ginga MacPhee

Again up in Kirkwall in my bunk as I lay
I heard him call out a distress and Mayday
I searched in the darkness but with no sign of him
Little did I know he had gone for a swim?

215

It took three boat club members his life then to save
We pulled him from the harbour and a watery grave
He repaid his debt with a meal for all three
My very grateful crewmember Ginga MacPhee

But when the going gets tough and it's all going wrong
That's when I'm thankful I have him along
He will pull out the stops and will never say die
Putting it simply he's my kind of Guy
So in 2007 when I head to the west
And I'm looking for crew I'll be wanting the best
He may have his faults but that's is ok by me
My valuable crewmember Ginga MacPhee

George Selvester July 2006

In **2007,** my son Steve and his girl friend wanted to cruise with us. I arranged for them to borrow *"Excalibur"*, a *Sunray 21* the same as *"Fat Sam"*. It had been damaged and was letting water in and for repairing the boat I could borrow it for two weeks. The work involved was quite extensive and I had to empty about 50 gallons of water from the cabin before I could even start the repairs the water had also affected the wiring so I rewired some of it so that they could have radio VHF etc.

There were 6 boats on the cruise altogether *"Evening Light"*, *"Rusharound"*, *"Norseman"*, *"Tunnag"* *"Fat Sam"* and *"Excalibur"*.

We set sail on Friday 6th July. The first problem we encountered was just before the Kessock Bridge when the engine on Excalibur packed in and I had to take it in tow as far as the sea locks at Clachnaharry.

There were many problems with the boat on the whole trip, which required my undivided attention all the time. We did have a good trip apart from those problems but I did not keep a detailed log of the trip I do recall all the places we visited. On leaving the canal we sailed to Loch Aline, Tobermory, Loch Na Droma Bhuidhe, Oban and Ballachulish, returning to Cromarty via the canal again.

Steve and Teleri aboard "*Excalibur*"

It was great to have my son and future daughter-in-law with me on that trip and I regret not having kept a log.

In September of **2007,** the club had a "long weekend cruise"; Danny Coutts was short of crew and asked if I would be his crew for the weekend on his recent acquisition "*La'Acushla*" a 30 ft Arpege.

There were four boats going, the others being "*Rusharound*" a 31 ft Jeanneau Rush, with owner skipper Willie Smeaton and a crew of Bill Paterson, " "*Evening Light*" with Gwyn Phillips, crewed by Neil Brooker, and "*Norseman*" with Peter Baxter and Lorraine.

We left Cromarty in the late afternoon on Friday and sailed straight for Lossiemouth in a good westerly wind arriving at 2100, the last boat in was Willie and with the tide ebbing he missed the "gate" to get in and had to tie up on the ladder at the entrance until he had enough water. We all now retired to the local pub, the Ferry Boat Inn, until we could bring "*Rusharound*" into the harbour with the rest of the fleet.

On the Saturday morning we set sail for Helmsdale in a very brisk force 6 six westerly, it was excellent sailing and we made good time across the Moray Firth.

Danny had made me a breakfast before we left and unfortunately gave me a "white" roll which always gives me heartburn.

About halfway to Helmsdale I was lying on the low side of the cockpit, suffering badly from the heartburn.

Danny said *"are you sure it is heartburn?"* I said I was sure it was, he then said, *"if it is a heart attack, can I have your Dubarry boots?"*...A friend indeed!!!

The following day, the weather was so bad we had to leave the boats at Helmsdale and getting the bus home we returned the next weekend to bring them home.

2008

The transatlantic trip

The idea to buy a boat from Florida had been in Gwyn Phillips' head for several years. He had spoken of it many times on our club cruises and although I never doubted that he would, in time, fulfil this dream; it came sooner than I had anticipated.

In 2006, he had again raised the issue and as usual I listened with interest but this time he seemed a bit more positive, from a personal point of view I did not want it to be in 2006 as my financial plans were all due to come to fruition a year later (November 2007 my mortgage would be finished) and I was keen to be one of his crew.

As luck would have it (for me at least) the plan for 2006 was to prove fruitless and the season ended with no more talk of Atlantic trips. He brought it up yet again in 2007,
This time I listened even more closely than before. By the end of the sailing season of that year Gwyn's plans were well underway, he had booked a flight to the States to look at a boat and was speaking with more confidence than he had done in the past.

By October of 2007 he had returned from the exploratory trip and although he had not liked the boat he had originally gone out to see, the advert had promised a boat with *"Two State Rooms"*, he phoned us to tell it was in fact a boat with *"two rooms in a state"*. However, whilst he was still over there he found another and arranged to view it, this one he did like! A "Hunter Legend" 40ft and well equipped, he immediately ordered a survey with the intention of buying.
November (the month my Mortgage ended!) saw a flurry of activity with the results of the Survey being positive and he set about recruiting his crew.

Bill Paterson had always been in Gwyn's thoughts as they are neighbours in Rosemarkie. Thankfully he then asked me in the presence of my wife Lilly, who at first was not keen on the idea of me being away for a two-month period, but she eventually agreed.

Neil Brooker, who had often sailed on the club cruises as crew to Gwyn, was asked to bring the total number of the crew to four and he readily agreed to be part of this new adventure.

When the crewmembers are examined closely, it became apparent that they were not chosen by accident, the skills of all of the members compliment each other giving a very competent crew for this undertaking with a combined sea time experience approaching *Two Hundred Years.*

The fact that they are all mates is an added bonus, even if two were pensioners and the other two getting very close.

The question we must now ask is: *after two months living in each others pockets will they be mates on their return?*

An interesting point here is that another mate of ours, Alex Davidson, who lived in Cromarty for fifteen years and was made an honorary member of the club before going home to Canada, is joining in Neil's place from Miami to Bermuda, Neil being unable, through his work commitments, to join us until then.

Alex was a sprightly 70 years old, which made him the senior aboard. He said he couldn't go any further than Bermuda as he felt he would probably have had a bellyful of us by then

When arranging all the finer details it suddenly came to our notice that we had to have Visas to enter USA. The reason for this being that we had no return ticket and could not show a port of departure.

Gwyn arranged for interviews at the American Embassy in London to which three of us had to attend, Gwyn, Bill and myself, this turned out to be a nuisance but as it was necessary we resigned ourselves to the chore.

We arrived at the Embassy on 24th January 2008 stood outside for an hour then sat inside the Embassy for a further two hours before the interview (which lasted around thirty seconds!) and we were granted the Visas which would be sent out within five days (charging us a further £14 each for return of our passports).

All in all, with days off work, flights, meals, rail tickets, taxi fares and tube fares and special delivery charges for the return of our passports, the day cost well in excess of £400. Fortunately for Bill and me, Gwyn picked up the Lions Share of the costs.

The trip is on!

We would fly to Florida 1st May 2008, make the boat ready for the trip, provision her and set sail for the UK on 6th May.

We were about to embark upon our epic journey:
Not exactly *"Jason and the Argonauts"*, more like *"Jester and the forget-a-lots"*

In March of **2008** (the same month my mother died) I was given an offer from an old friend of mine. Jock Wingate was selling his *Westerly Griffon "Heart of Gold"* and as I was approaching age of retirement, I had an endowment coming to maturity in the July of that year.

This along with the sale of *"Fat Sam"* would allow me to purchase this wonderful boat. I discussed it with Lilly and she agreed that it would be a good investment. By the start of the 2008 season I was the proud owner of this beautiful boat.

Before I could go with Gwyn to collect his boat from Miami I had to get *"Heart of Gold"* from Findhorn or I would have to pay berthing costs for the whole time I was away. In early April, Jock had arranged for the boat to be craned in and it would be lying on a pontoon, waiting for me to sail it over to Cromarty.

My sister Maureen was over from Australia and when I told her I was going to collect the boat from Findhorn, she volunteered herself and Lilly to accompany me.

When the weekend arrived, the forecast was not too great, it would be blowing force 7 from the west and the trip home would be "lumpy. "

I tried to dissuade them from going but they seemed determined. Lynda and Raymond (our daughter and son-in-law) had agreed to take us over. As we drove over I again pointed out that it would be no picnic but they would have none of it.

When we got down to the boat Lynda and Raymond wanted to look over the boat and as they did I again suggested that it might be better if Mo and Lilly went back with them.

They were still adamant, just before leaving, I said, *"when I sail over that sand bar, there is no way I am turning back!"* We had only gone for a couple of miles when Maureen started showing signs of sickness and Lilly, although not being sick, was certainly not happy. The trip back for them which took over 4 hours must have been sheer hell and as we sailed through the Sutors, Maureen with a plastic bag still held up under her chin said *"Do you call this f****** enjoyment?"* I stopped myself from saying `"I told you so!"*

My Westerly Griffon *"Heart of Gold"*

Off to Miami

The flight to Florida was reasonable and we landed at Sanford Airport where Gwyn had arranged one-way car hire for the drive down to Miami.
I noticed the temperature immediately, I could live with this!
We stopped for a bite to eat on the way and to stretch our legs. We also had a fuel stop. We arrived at the boat in the late afternoon. We threw our gear on board and went for some provisions, before settling down at night for a few drinks before retiring.

"Sassie Lassie" at Miami

The following week would see us put in a full days work every day, preparing the boat for the trip. There was no real major work needing done and if it required a specialist Gwyn had a guy who regularly came round with his van full of special tools to complete the job.

Most of the work we did was on running rigging, and sails and we all paid particular attention to the life saving equipment on board. We would take mornings drawing up lists of required items then the afternoon fulfilling these lists at stores whether it be grocery stores or marina chandlery.

Where the boat was moored, was owned by an elderly couple and they allowed us the use of their swimming pool.

We ate out quite regularly at a restaurant at the local boat club or as often as not the local "Subway" shop. Alex had joined after the first couple of days but his baggage had gone missing and we had to return several times to the airport to see if it had turned up. Two days before we departed the bags turned up. Alex was sailing as "cook" until we reached Bermuda and he would fly home to Canada from there.

Eventually the day arrived when we set sail for Scotland; the trip down through Miami Harbour, under a flyover with only a few inches clearance from the top of the mast was interesting to say the least.

Once clear of the harbour and heading for the open sea we could look back and see "Miami Beach."

Gwyn had worked out a rota/watch system. Each member of the sailing crew would have a "watch" of three hours; whoever was going off watch would brief his relief on the course he had been steering, as per Gwyn's passage plan.

When coming off watch the retiring watch keeper would record: current position, distance covered, weather at time of change over and include his own remarks.

This system ensures that most eventualities were covered and the maximum information was passed on.

Before coming on watch, each member would read the previous entry then ask the current situation from whoever he was relieving.

Me in the Gulf Stream (on the boat of course)

Gwyn, being the skipper had the final decision to make on any contentious issue and could be summoned by simply stamping your foot on the deck as his cabin was immediately below the steering position

The local radio transmits where the "Gulf Stream" is expected to be, I did not know it shifted daily!
We listened and understood it to be 4.5 miles offshore from where we were. I had heard about the change in colour of the water but never imagined how beautiful it would be. The waters off the coast of Miami are a terrific blue colour but when you enter the Gulf Stream it shows up as wonderful light blue/green, almost impossible to describe.
The speed is something else I had never imagined; it can be as high as 3.5 knots carrying you in a north-easterly direction.
The trip at the start was enjoyable because of the sunshine. As we approached the top of the Florida straights having achieved 150 miles in the first 24 hrs we were elated.
We had been working 3hrs on and 6hrs off with Alex doing the cooking and cleaning and all was working well.
The watch system was working well and everyone was getting the sleep they needed. When we were around 90 miles north of the Bahamas, I was on watch, during daylight hours when I saw something that disturbed me a little. I shouted to Bill who was still awake and moving around, "*is Gwyn awake at*

the moment?" Bill said that he thought he was, I said, *"tell him I need his advice!"*
Gwyn appeared at the hatchway to ask what I wanted,
I said, "*What do I do about that?"*
Gwyn, on seeing the same thing as me, a twister drawing seawater and God knows what else up into the skies, said "*alter course to avoid it*" I asked "*which way?"* He replied "*Start the engine and go to port* ". This I started to do but it seemed as though the spout was following us, we moved about for some time before deciding on a course that would take us clear of the danger. It passed by a few hundred yards away and we breathed a sigh of relief.

For a few days after that life was all sweetness and light it was good sailing and we got ourselves into the routine of the watch system.

At one point when we were at least 400 miles from the nearest land a little bird visited us. I am not too sure of the kind but it looked a little like a yellowhammer.

It stayed with us for a couple of days and got really brave flying in and out of the cabin eating the scraps we would leave for it and at one point was perched on Gwyn's big toe looking at him.

It did attempt to fly off a couple of times, but returned to the boat immediately.

I got up for my watch early one morning and found the poor little thing on the deck; it had been squashed to death. Someone must have stood on it, but no-one would admit it.

We experienced some electric storms and I don't mind telling you I was a little afraid, the sheet lightning seemed to turn the darkest night into broad daylight momentarily; I could not help but think how vulnerable I was with my hands on the steel steering wheel.

I liked the boat's lines and the accommodation below was superb, as were the navigation aids. The chart plotter I also found to be a great asset but I found it very difficult to get into a comfortable position when at the helm. This problem got even worse when we hit storm winds at around 200 miles south west of Bermuda. We were coping well with it at first, but when it came round to the west and the huge seas were hitting our port quarter all the time, the boat was yawing terribly.

The winds were still increasing and although we had reefed earlier, we now had to take the sails down altogether the main was hard work but the foresail relatively easy, except for the fact it would not pull away completely.

Now with no sails at all, we were still doing over 5 knots on bare poles.

The foresail still had about a foot that was not furled and was in danger of being ripped by the wind tearing at it. Gwyn attempted to pull the roller reefing in further with the winch, but it was already tight, his efforts pulled the furling line right off the drum and the sail started to unfurl open and fill, not a position we wanted to be in!

Bill took the helm while Gwyn and I tried to recover the sail, all we could do was to let go the halyard and pull it down, gather it and lash it to the guard rails as best we could.

With the wind staying with us for a long time, I asked Gwyn if I should call Bermuda Harbour Radio on the satellite phone, to let them know we were out here and to see if they could update us on the weather situation.

Gwyn agreed and I dialled the number, I got through to a woman who was so "matter of fact" in her replies. I said "*we are a British Registered Yacht currently 150 miles south west of Bermuda and I am asking for info on a storm we are in"* she said *"there is no-one here that can give you that information"* I had in my head a vision of her painting her nails as I was talking to her. I asked she could give me the number of someone who could help me and this she did.

I phoned the second number and got a man who was exactly the same in his attitude, he was more interested in whether or not we had safety equipment on board and asked for the number of our EPIRB. I explained that all I wanted at this stage was an update of the storms we were experiencing. He asked me to give him our current position in Lat/Long, which I did; his next statement almost floored me. He said, *"There are storms forecast for that area!"* I yelled down the phone, *"we are in the storms!"*

Realising the futility of speaking to these people, we went back to trying to ride out the storm. The boat was obviously capable of surviving so we had to deal with it as the experienced sailors we are, no-one else could help us out here.

The next 24 hrs were energy sapping, we started the motor to try and help the yawing and we went to 3 hrs on the helm, 3 hrs on standby, remaining on hand in the cockpit to assist the helmsman, should the need arise, and 3 hrs off. The 3 hrs off was laughable, because it was next to impossible to sleep with the movement of the boat.

Alex had not moved out of the forepeak since the storms had hit us. He did access the forward heads (toilet) but really spent he time rolling from one side to the other and was unable to get out and make any meals.

I strapped myself to the bar at the front of the cooker and was able to reach the fridge, where I managed to rustle up four bowls of salad with tinned tuna with it, not the best of meals, but I was famished.

When on the helm in those conditions, the concentration is such that; you tend not to see anything except the task in hand. When you are sitting as stand-by in the cockpit you get a chance to see the size of the waves and it kind of focuses the mind.

I now had time to see the waves and believe me they were enormous. When at the top of the wave looking down it was spectacular, it makes you feel so insignificant in the whole scheme of things.

We kept this watch system up for the duration until we arrived in St George's Harbour, but when we were around 12 hrs out of Bermuda we experienced a full "knock down" a huge rogue curling wave seemed to grab the boat, slew it to port and as the wave broke, knocked us over completely onto our starboard side.

Bill was on the helm and I was on standby, with Gwyn resting below, Bill held his position with having a good grip on the wheel, I was thrown out of the boat into the sea but had my lifeline on so stayed attached to the boat.

My lifejacket inflated as soon as I hit the water and as I came to the surface with foam all around, I could see immediately in front of me the stainless steel curved bar, which was ahead of the wheel. I grabbed a hold of that knowing (Or was I hoping?) that the boat would right itself again. When it did right I found myself standing right next to Bill.

We had to suffer fully inflated lifejackets from there to Bermuda.

Gwyn, who had been resting on the port berth in the main saloon, was thrown across the boat, clattering his legs against the compression post for the mast, which resulted in severe bruising, had he been lying the other way round, it would have been his head. Alex simply rolled from one side to the other in the forepeak.

The after lockers in the cockpit had been left unlatched and water got through them into the cabins, as we were almost submerged, wetting everyone's gear.

We were now a sorry looking lot, completely soaked through, with nothing dry to change into and wearing fully inflated lifejackets.

From there to St George's Harbour seemed like days instead of hours and we were so relieved to see the Gibb's Hill Lighthouse at the southern end of Bermuda.

We sailed along the coast staying about five miles off until we could make our approach to St George's, which is at the north end of the island.

For entering the harbour Gwyn gave us our specific duties, which reminded me of my RN days. Gwyn was navigating and spotting marks and lights, I was the radioman, in constant communication with Bermuda Harbour Radio (BHR) and Bill was on the helm.

The passage in is quite tricky, but BHR had us on radar most of the way in and I could talk to them. We dropped anchor in the quarantine area at around 0200. We were all so tired, yet we opened a couple of bottles and celebrated having completed the first leg of 900 miles.

Once we had cleared customs I had to talk to Gwyn, my ankles were swollen to almost the same size as the rest of my lower leg. My arthritis had been made a lot worse by bracing myself to steer the boat and I felt I was unable to continue. Neil Brooker was joining us in a few days, which would have brought the compliment of sailors to four.

With me now leaving it would mean a lot more work for the others; they would have to split the cleaning and cooking duties and take their turn on watch. To have four doing this is hard enough and now I was letting them down. I was really sorry but I could not put up with the pain any longer.

Alex and I booked into a hotel and I arranged to fly home two days later. We did meet up with the guys a couple of times before we flew out. They stayed a full week before sailing from there to the Azores.

On my return to UK I took over the job of supplying the weather information to the boat via the satellite phone.

When I returned home I took it easy for a week, I attended the doctor about my ankles but the condition is virtually untreatable, apart from anti-inflammatory and painkillers.

I was advised not to stop or they would simply seize up altogether, so I went back to work and sailed my new boat "*Heart of Gold*"

I entered the Moray Firth Cruiser Race with my new boat and I won!

Ginga was absolutely delighted, I must admit that I was quite happy too.

When "Sassie Lassie" arrived from Miami there was a good welcoming party for them at Cromarty. I sailed round to the Inverness Firth with "*Heart of Gold*" to escort them home, the Lifeboat with Danny Coutts as the cox came out and escorted them into Cromarty Firth.

"*Sassie Lassie*" went straight to her mooring and once they were ready I went alongside her and acted as the taxi into the harbour where all the friends and relations of the crew were waiting to cheer them in.

It was a truly remarkable achievement for them and I was glad to have been a part of it.

In Home Waters once again

In **2009** we went Orkney again. For some strange reason I do not have a detailed log of this trip but remember it all anyway.

We had the annual cruise meeting where lots of people said they would come but eventually the numbers were whittled down to three usual boats, me and Ginga on *"Heart of Gold,"* Bill Paterson and Bob Bull on *"Tunnag"* and Gwyn and Willie Smeaton on *"Sassie Lassie"*

We sailed out on the Saturday morning with not much wind at all. The first stop was to be Wick, which would take us the best part of twelve hours.

"Heart of Gold" taken from *"Sassie Lassie"*

With the complete lack of wind we had to motor most of the way. The trip was pretty uneventful until we reached Clyth Ness when the fog that we had been seeing on the horizon suddenly closed in with limited visibility, less than 100 yards. We would have to complete the remainder of the leg using GPS, what did we do without it?

When the fog had closed in *"Sassie Lassie"* and *"Heart of Gold"* were abreast of each other but around 100yds apart. We continued to communicate with each other via the VHF but could no longer see each other. Bill called to tell us his position and asked me where I was, I told him I was 5 miles from the waypoint for Wick, Gwyn said that was where he was too.

When around an hour later I called to tell the other boats I had reached the waypoint, Gwyn replied that he too was at the waypoint. I turned onto the heading given in the Almanac for the approach to Wick and asked Ginga to go forward and keep a sharp lookout and to listen for anything untoward and yell if something is there.
I was down to 2 knots in case we saw something and out of the fog on my starboard bow appeared the north cardinal mark, which marks the end of the old breakwater; we were on the wrong side of it! I turned quickly to starboard to get it on my port side and just as I passed it I suddenly saw Gwyn ahead

of me, fortunately Gwyn saw me. He too turned to starboard. I was now outside the cardinal so turned to port again to approach the harbour; at least we knew we were close.

The breakwater was the next thing we saw and slipped round the end of it into he safety of the harbour, finding the pontoons was easy and within minutes we were tied up alongside. Gwyn appeared a minute or two after us and he too moored up. Twenty minutes later Bill arrived, we were all now safe.

The following morning, the fog had gone but there was still no wind so we set of under power yet again. The distance to Duncansby Head is just over twelve miles and we have calculated the best time to be there and all three of us are now "old hands" at crossing this stretch of water.

I received a call from Gwyn to tell me that he thought there was too much steam coming out of my exhaust and not enough water. I asked him to keep an eye on me when crossing the firth in case my engine stopped.

I positioned my boat so that if the engine did stop the tide would be carrying me toward "Sassie Lassie" and he could get a line to me if need be.

Just after we passed the Lother Rock the wind got up and I was able to sail the remainder of the way to

Hoxa Head then round to the entrance of St Margaret's Hope.
The shelter in this bay is excellent as is the pub ashore where we enjoyed fish and chips washed down with a pint of lager.

"Tunnag" and *"Heart of Gold"*, St Margaret's Hope

I discussed my overheating problem and figured it could only be the impeller in the water pump that was faulty, I do have a spare one but it is in my garage at home.

Next morning there was an excellent sailing wind from the northeast, which would mean a very good sail all the way to Stromness. I was ahead of the others and at one point I called to Gwyn to ask why they were stopped; he had fouled a long line, he had been sailing at 6 knots when it slipped under his keel but fouled on the rudder. They had to take down their sails and get a knife to cut the rope free. Within five minutes he radioed to say they were fine and getting underway again. The rest of the trip to Stromness was uneventful.

I contacted the Volvo dealer in Kirkwall and gave him the numbers needed to order my part. He asked me to ring back later which I did and was told that the part would take three days to get here.

Bob Bull, Bill's crew member had been having difficulties and had spoken to me to say that he was of a mind to go home but did not want to let Bill down. I said that it should be Bill he should be having this discussion with. The three days waiting time was an eternity and I was pleased that the other guys stayed with me to wait for the part and Stromness is a nice town.

We also visited Kirkwall by bus and took in a couple of places there.

On the day before my part was due to arrive I was lying in my bed in the early morning when I received a text message from Bob Bull telling me that he had caught the early ferry to the mainland and asked if I would tell Bill.

What a strange way of communicating.

Next day I got the bus to Kirkwall and picked up the part I needed and went straight back to the boat to fit it. Within an hour the engine was running and the water flow was a lot better. We were now too late to continue with the original plans so a meeting was held to discuss our options.

I had never been to Longhope and suggested we go there; all agreed so we set sail on a course that would take us down between Cava and Hoy then Fara and Hoy and into Longhope.

We had a word with the Lifeboat cox who is a friend of Danny Coutts then we retired to the only pub in the area.

During our time in the pub we got talking to some locals and on hearing that Bill was single handed going over the Pentland Firth on the return journey one of them volunteered to crew Bill all the way back to Cromarty, if he could bring his dog.

He agreed he would be down at the harbour at 0700 ready for the off.

True to his word, Richard Smith and his dog Robbie were there at the appointed time.

The passage timings had been calculated from the instructions in the Clyde Cruising Club Pilot book which said that the tide turned in the Pentland at Aberdeen High Water minus 4 hours 30 minutes.

On that day, we calculated that it would turn eastwards at around 9.00am, so we left ourselves an hour and a half to get from Long Hope, around Cantick Head, and up to Aith Head where the guide said we should begin the crossing.

All went well, apart from a slight worry when we were a good bit ahead of time and slowed down to three knots approaching Cantick Head, at the appointed hour, we pointed the bows due south as Aith Hope opened before us.

The passage across the Firth, between Swona and Stroma, took only an hour and forty minutes, with our speed over the ground approaching 10 knots at times, before we were swept around Duncansby Head and heading for Wick.

This time the entrance to Wick Harbour was easy in excellent visibility and calm seas.

The following morning we sailed home.

Findochty to Inverness

September 2009

Neil Jenkins, the prospective owner of "*Jenna*" a 26 ft Westerly Griffon, had contacted me through the Westerly Owners Association to discuss the pros and cons of this type of boat.

He and his wife, Tina, joined me aboard my Griffon, "*Heart of Gold*" one weekend in July and they were both so taken by the performance that he decided he would go and see the one for sale in Caley Brokerage, which was lying in Findochty.

I did not hear from him for some considerable time after that initial contact and was surprised to hear that he had contacted Gwyn in his capacity as a delivery company for assistance in sailing his new acquisition from Findochty to his home port of Lochinver. As I had the first contact with Neil, Gwyn asked if I would complete the first leg of its journey to Inverness.

I readily agreed and was picked up from home on a Tuesday night and after dropping off Tina, his wife, by car at Muirton Basin in Inverness, we arrived at Findochty around 1900.

Neil had told me that the boat came complete with a survey and I assumed it would be in pretty reasonable condition. My first impression of the boat was not the best, many of the deck fittings were secured by mild steel nuts and bolts and brown lines of rust from these fittings gave it the look of a sadly neglected boat.

I was to learn that the previous owner was a farmer, which would explain the boarding ladder which was obviously recovered from an old combine harvester, it was worse than useless, as it was secured to the push pit (after Guard rail) with a rope which would be well out of reach for anyone unlucky enough to be trying to get on board from the water.

I had agreed to fit a new impeller to the water pump and new fuel filters this I did, before we went for an evening meal at the local hotel. During the meal, I explained the passage plan to an attentive Neil and Tina. I planned to leave the harbour at 0530 so suggested it might be a good idea to turn in early.

Back at the boat I had the forward cabin whilst the owners slept in the main cabin. Many Westerly's of this age normally have drooping headlining, not this one, it had been ripped out leaving the broken down foam stuck to the fibreglass, still the bed was OK and I drifted off to sleep.

Wednesday 0500: I awoke to the sounds of activity in the main cabin and after confirming that they were dressed, I emerged to have a cup of coffee before setting sail. It was obvious that neither Neil or Tina were used to sailing with the tide as they seemed to take for ever to get themselves organised, I became increasingly more agitated as the clock ticked by.

0600: I practically threw Tina and her belongings off the boat and slipped the lines before we became tide locked in the harbour, as the tide was now falling quite rapidly.

We were well clear of the harbour when the first problem arose, the engine spluttered to a halt. We quickly rolled out the foresail and although it was keeping us moving, it was a very tired looking sail, we then hoisted the main, to find that it was in a worse condition than the foresail.

I left Neil at the helm and went below to determine the fault with the engine, it had been drawing air at one of the filters and I adjusted the seating on the bowl, bled the system and fired her up.

With barely a slight breeze, right on our nose, I suggested we keep the engine going but it cut out again and I found that it had still been taking air.

I quickly found the problem and bled it again, to find that it was running quite smoothly.

About two hours later, as we passed the mouth of Lossiemouth harbour, the overheating alarm came on so we had to put in to the harbour, to try and determine the problem.

I removed the thermostat housing to find that it was working fine but the whole thing was blocked with a black sticky mess. On closer examination the waterway was blocked by an old piece of impeller and after removing that, clearing the waterways and started to replace everything, I then discovered that the "O" ring was completely useless so went in search of a garage to source one. The lad at the garage also gave me some jointing compound to replace the housing.

By the time we got all this done it was close to 1000, we had done 12.5 nautical miles, only a quarter of the way to Inverness, so the passage plan was out of the window.

Trying to make the best of a bad day, we set off again with renewed hope. All went well until around mid-day when the overheating alarm starting buzzing again and Neil could also see water in the bottom of the boat, he lifted the floorboards to see that we were indeed taking water, I asked for the handle to the bilge pump and started pumping... ...nothing! The pump was not working!

I told Neil that the only thing to do now was get a bucket and start baling, as soon as he started this he told me that the water was warm. A quick check in the engine compartment revealed that where there should have been a coolant drain cock on the engine block, there was an old bolt covered in sealant jammed into the hole and held in by a block of wood against the injection pump.

We were halfway between the South Sutor and Burghead at this point and I decided to make straight for Cromarty, Neil spent the rest of the trip baling and I spent the rest of the trip wishing I were on my own boat.

We did manage to get to Cromarty at around 1400 and Neil asked "what are you going to do now?" "I am off to the pub!" said I.

The following weekend, I did a temporary repair to the block and we made the uneventful trip from Cromarty to Caley Marina where an engineer would complete the repair before "*Jenna*" continued her journey through the canal and onto Lochinver, not with me aboard, I might add.

The **2010** cruise started with great hopes but these hopes were looking very dodgy within the first few days. There was a good number of boats had committed to going.

"Sassie Lassie," "Octopus," "Havana Breeze," "Drumlin," "Heart of Gold" "Tunnag" and *"Les trois frères.*

Danny Coutts was already on the west coast with *"La'Acushla"* and planned joining us at Oban. Gwyn's intention was to cruise with us as far north of Ardnamurchan Point as we could achieve and when we turned to come home he would continue to Lochinver where he would leave his boat for a few days (Neil Jenkins lives up there and he would keep his eye on the boat) while Gwyn went to his daughter's graduation in Glasgow.

The first indication we had that there might be a problem was when Danny phoned me from Oban to say that he with his boat *"La'Acushla"* had been storm bound in Kerrera marina for the last 3 days.

"Sassie Lassie" "Octopus" and *"Havana Breeze"* were already into the canal system by early on the Friday and would wait for the remainder of the fleet to catch up with them.

The Cromarty boats were due to leave on the Saturday to enter the canal in the afternoon when they would link up with the others.

"Tunnag" and *"Les trois frères* left at 0900 and I waited for David Price with his boat *"Drumlin".*

A call from David at 1030 told me he was running late and to go without him, he would try to catch us up.
When I sailed past Chanonry light I could hear Bill and Bob chatting via VHF, the engine on Bob's boat was giving him problems and he was putting into Avoch harbour to try to repair. I waited until he had managed to get into the harbour and then set off again for Clachnaharry Sea Lock.

I received another call on VHF to say that "*Drumlin*" was now on his way and was in the Inverness Firth. Bill was just ahead of me entering the sea lock and we were soon with the others, as a group we now set about going up the Muirton flight, "*Drumlin*" had indeed caught us up and steamed straight into the "Locking up" with the rest of us.

From there we had no hold ups steaming in a line through Tomnahurich bridge and Dochgarroch lock.

The problem that now arose was that the wind from the southwest had increased considerably and as we entered Loch Ness it was right "on the nose" and the waves on the loch, although short and not very steep, still managed to slow the smaller boats down, I was only managing to make 2 knots with the engine working at almost full throttle.

I tried to persevere for about 30 minutes then radioed the fleet to say I was returning to Dochgarroch for the night. As soon as I made that call and turned back "*Drumlin*" and "Tunnag" followed suit. The rest of the fleet being heavier than us kept going and did manage to make Fort Augustus that night.

The lock keeper at Dochgarroch would not allow us to stop at the top side of the lock overnight so we had to drop down again, this would mean we would not get an early start in the morning.

At 0815 next morning ,we were locking up again and headed back out onto Loch Ness, the weather, although not quite as bad as yesterday was still making headway painfully slow and it took us almost five hours to cover the 21 miles of the Loch.

On arrival at Fort Augustus, there was a load of boats coming down the flight so it would be late before we got to the top.

The others were already at the top waiting for us and by the time we eventually made it up the flight, it was too late to go anywhere else. We retired to the local Royal British Legion Club for refreshments.

The trip from there to Banavie, is normally quite trouble free and so it proved the following morning as we all moored up at the top of Neptune's Staircase and we were informed by the lock keepers that unless we would commit to going to sea, we could not go down the flight. I made the remark that anyone who chose to go to sea in this weather forecast needs "Committed!"

For three full days we sat and listened to the forecast, which at no time seemed to show any improvement. On the morning of the fourth day we held a skippers meeting and the decision was made to cut our losses and head home. Turning round now would mean we could exit the canal within the eight-day pass and incur no more charges.

We waited until the afternoon to sail back toward Fort Augustus and by the time we reached Laggan Locks the wind was ferocious. The gates here were broken, one gate, and the lock keeper was unwilling to let us attempt entering the lock with such a strong following wind, someone may get damaged. We resigned ourselves to an overnight here. There was a good party aboard "Octopus" which went on into the early hours of the morning. Before we left next morning John Munro, our club secretary met up with us as he was heading south, we wished him the best of luck and started out for home.

On arriving at the top of Fort Augustus locks the wind was causing havoc with all the boats, "*Sassie Lassie*" sustained damage to its pulpit when the wind caught the boat and drove it into the pier. I had moored alongside Gwyn and now decided to move to a space at the lock gates and gave a demonstration of how to moor a boat at 5 knots going astern. I slipped "Heart of Gold" into the tight space and engaged ahead at the precise time to bring her to a halt without hint of any damage. All the club members gave me a standing ovation; I took a bow and said, "*If you've got it, flaunt it!*"

The remainder of the trip home was without incident unless you count my engine failing at Chanonry Point on the last leg home and having to be taken in tow by *"Drumlin"*

Once home I had found the cylinder head gasket had failed, I took the head off the engine to get it skimmed and fitted a new gasket. The job took me several days and I had a fair bit of bother to get the timing right again and the tappet settings but after a lot of trial and error I managed to get it running again: Job done, running again, roll on next summer!

Rothesay to Cromarty

Finlay Crawford had wanted a boat for a number of years and had been actively looking for one. A Mitchell 31 appeared in "Find a Fishing Boat" and after a few phone calls and a visit to see the boat "Susie Anna" he agreed to buy it.

Once the deal was done he decided he needed an experienced sailor/navigator to help him bring it home to Cromarty and asked me to accompany him.

Monday 2nd August 2010.

Fin had arranged to pick me up at 0900 in Cromarty and then pick up his mate Martin from Culbokie, Martin would drive Fin's car back from Rothesay.

We were on the main A9 at Tore by 0945 and heading south, hoping to arrive at around 1400. The first problem was that the engine management in his car, told us his oil was getting low, so we pulled into Aviemore, to buy a grossly overpriced can of lube oil.

The next stop was Perth, for a cup of coffee, a pie and a toilet stop, then on the road again. Traffic was a little heavier than we anticipated and with the road works outside Cumbernauld slowing us further the "Tom-Tom" Sat Nav told us we would not be in Rothesay until 1445.

We caught the 1400 Ferry at Wemyss Bay in time to be over at the harbour for that expected time. When Fin presented himself at the door of the house he found that he had only sent a cheque for the deposit and the lady, quite rightly, would not release the boat keys until the balance was paid.

Fin then frantically visited the local branch of his bank and tried to arrange for the funds to be released, very time consuming and a little frustrating.

Martin and I sat in the car thinking we might be driving all the way home again.

With the money now in his hands we returned to the house, over an hour later than planned paid the money and quickly set of down to the waterside to launch the dinghy. Fin set off for the boat lying at anchor while Martin and I went round to the marina where we offloaded all the gear allowing Martin to catch the next Ferry at 1645.

I stood by the gear watching the ferry arrive and hoping that Fin would have the sense to wait until the ferry docked before attempting to enter the harbour, I was relieved to see him take a turn around, allowing the ferry to dock before coming in, alas he was 20 seconds too soon as the red lights were still showing.

The harbour master came down to have a word with him. He had owned the boat for all of ten minutes and was already on a warning!

We loaded all the gear aboard and made her ready for sea before retiring to the local for a few beers.

The original plan was to sail round the top of Kyle through "Burnt Isles" but as there was a tidal gate, which would mean waiting until around 0900, we decided to sail round the bottom of Kyle which would allow us to start at 0500.

Tuesday 3rd August 2010.

We were up at around 0445 and after a quick cup of tea we set sail just after 0500. The wind was very light from the west but due to increase as the day progressed. We made excellent time and although the trip to the south would mean an extra 3 miles onto the journey the decision was the right call. Crossing Inch Marnock water was a little bumpy, but once we were into Lower Loch Fyne in the lee of the land, the water flattened out again allowing us to make a steady seven knots and we arrived at Ardrisahaig at 1005.

Another boat arrived at the same time as us and we thought it would be assistance going through the canal as we could share the work off opening the lock gates, all done by hand, unfortunately they seemed to be in no hurry to transverse the canal. Two boats coming the other way, one single handed, were of a similar "laid back" attitude and held us up even more that we wanted.

We eventually shook them off and made our way through with no assistance from anyone else.

Fin stayed on the boat, as I had managed to take a chip out of his bow on the first lock, and I did the lock gates. I don't mind admitting that the task is difficult for a 67-year-old arthritic!

However we managed to get most of the way through before we ran out of time at 1700 at a point called Bellanoch Bridge. As there was no pub here, we were a bit disappointed, but after a bite to eat, some of Fin's precooked Venison, a shower and a couple of glasses of wine we were quite content.

I started to rework my figures for the next day to get round "Dorus Mhor" and was alarmed to discover that we could not cross at the time I had first said, 1000, it would be afternoon before we could round the point. The more I looked at it the worse it became, I said I would leave it until I felt fresh in the morning.

As we were both so tired we hit the sack at around 2100.

Wednesday 4th August 2010.

I slept right through to 0600 and made my way over to the showers, on my return Fin trotted off for a shower as I made breakfast. With breakfast out of the way I got the almanac out and looked at tide times, etc for setting off.

Fin had already resigned himself to waiting until the afternoon, but was delighted, when I told him that my first calculations were indeed correct and we should be at "Dorus Mhor" for 1000.

As soon as the lock keeper appeared we were on our way again and cleared the canal at Crinan by 0945.

The distance form the canal to the sound of Jura is only 4NM so the journey to there was only around twenty minutes. As soon as we entered the sound, the tide picked us up and increased our speed by over a knot and kept increasing as we motored up to the sound of Luing.

We carried the tide all the way up past, Luing then Seil until we were level with the Kererra, arriving there at Low Water Oban, this would mean that the tide would now be in our favour up Loch Linnhe and through Corran Narrows.

Salad sandwiches for lunch were made by Fin and went down very well

The day's trip was uneventful and quite pleasant with the light winds. The only thing I found a bit irritating was the noise of the 6-cylinder ford thumping away all day. At one point I suggested that Fin might want to call his new acquisition "Foisy Nucker.

As we approached Fort William I radioed Corpach to find that the lock gates were open for us, we motored straight in and were tied up in the basin by 1655.

After a meal on board, we wandered up the town to find a pub and shared a few beers with the yacht that had entered the basin after us. They had hired the Jeanneau 42 "Skua" for a week and had entered the basin as a safe haven berth for the night. They asked for ideas for an overnight in Loch Linnhe before returning the boat the next again day I suggested Kentallen Bay or Loch Aline.

We returned to the boats after the "last orders" were shouted in the bar, the crew from the yacht had ordered a Chinese carry out for delivery after they returned on board. Fin and I returned to "Susie Anna" turning in as soon as we were on board.

Thursday 5th August 2010

We arranged to start moving as soon as we could, but had to wait for the Banavie Lock Down. We went up the first lock into the reach and waited at the rail bridge for the boats coming out of the "Neptune's Staircase" then the bridge opened, to reveal the boats emerging from the bottom lock. One of our club members, Peter Baxter was in the lock with his boat "*Red Ruth*" a Rustler 42 he and his partner Lorraine were taking it down to Falmouth for the winter before heading for the Mediterranean in spring of 2011.

Peter seemed to take forever to come out of the lock and the others behind him were also taking their time.

We were anxious to get up the flight and away to Fort Augustus to get the last lock down of the day so as to be ready for going up Loch Ness first thing in the morning.

There was another boat with us in the lock a Seal 28 "Trilogy" he was obviously in no hurry either and seemed to take great delight in taking his time into each lock. Even after we were clear of the staircase he hung back for the bridges and other locks adding unnecessary time to our travel. We eventually got clear of him and felt we were at last making a fair speed, this was not to last as we came upon another yacht at Laggan Locks, "*Hotspur*", a Leisure 23 SL, who was probably going as fast as he could but again we had to wait for him at Cullochy Lock for a further five minutes.

We asked the lock keeper to radio or phone ahead to Fort Augustus to let them know we wanted down the flight today. Again at Kytra we had to wait for "*Hotspur*" and the lock keeper there informed us that the last lock down of the day had already started at the flight. We had missed it by ten minutes!

After buying a fish supper and returning to the boat, Fin did a bit of fishing and I had a nap. At around 2000 we walked down to the Royal British Legion Club but as I was not feeling too great we left after only two drinks, I was in bed by 2130.

Friday 6th August 2010.

The first Lock down was scheduled for 0800, but in fact did not start until around 0820, as soon as we reached the bottom of the flight we motored out into Loch Ness and started on the last leg home, it took us three hours to travel up the Loch and as we approached Dochgarroch I tried to Radio the lock keeper, no answer.
On arriving at the lock he took us in and told us we had to wait for the "*Jacobite Queen*" to arrive, another ten minutes wasted!!

By the time we cleared that lock and pulled over so that the "Queen" could go first, then pushing our way past a bunch of "Caley Crushers" we tried to get to the Tomnahurich Bridge and through to Muirton. The Highland Council now dictate the opening times of bridges in and around Inverness so we had a 20 minute wait before the bridge opened. When we got to Muirton they staff were on their lunch break and we could not lock down until 1400, again they were 10 minutes late and seemed to relish holding us back.

Once through the basin we quickly went through the last two locks into the salt water again at 1515. The tide was just reaching slack water at low tide and we had a smooth passage under the bridge, passing Jock Wingate doing his Dolphin Tours just after the bridge. An uneventful passage from there to Cromarty arriving at 1745, we offloaded all my gear where Lilly met us at the harbour with the car and after helping Fin pick up a mooring in the bay I went home to the grandkids, a meal and a night in my own bed.

During the trip Fin asked lots of questions about navigation, rules of the road and general seamanship, I suggested some good reading for him and have agreed to give him more tuition on the navigation side during the winter. He is a practical, intelligent and responsible man and will make a good skipper.

I started the **2011** season with certain optimism that this year would be a good one. Looking back I realised this must have been one of the most confused seasons I can remember as far as weather is concerned.

The wind is either so strong that the seagulls are flying backwards or there is no wind at all. Sometimes we get both conditions in the same day. Such was the 2011 Moray Firth Cruiser Race,

Saturday 18th June.

The race has started at Findhorn from many years but was changed in 2010 to start and finish at Cromarty. I raced last year and was beaten by my very good friend Mike Burns in his *Folksong "Fram"*, this year I was out for revenge!

The start was a bit slow with very light winds and we all headed for the first mark at a sedate pace, just before any boat reached the mark, the wind dropped to no more than a whisper. I had allowed for the tide and it was now making and if I could just squeeze round this 1st mark before it strengthened I would be fine.
It looked like touch and go for a while and I was relieved to see the mark slide past my starboard side with a couple of feet to spare.

I now had the tide behind me to the next mark, I tried the spinnaker but it would fill and collapse several times before picking up just enough to keep driving me just a smidgeon faster than the tide.

The other boats behind me were toiling to make the 1st mark as the tide was now taking them away from it.

Once round the second mark the wind strengthened slightly and I was now on a bit of a reach. For the next two hours all the boats would find a little wind for a while then would all sit becalmed for a period.

My luck still held out and by the time I came to the second last mark before the finish line the wind had suddenly strengthened to a force 4 from the west.

From here to the finish line via Buss Bank Buoy (the last mark) is just over 5 miles and I completed it in 50 minutes.

I had line honours on all the three classes and I had won my class in the Moray Firth Cruiser Race for a third time, once with "*Fat Sam*" and now twice with "*Heart of Gold.* "

I was so far ahead of any other boat when I finished that I had time to go home and shower and change my clothes.

When I went to pick up my trophy at the prize giving in the pub, one of the other competitors remarked on my being smartly dressed "*if you did not keep all that fancy gear aboard your boat might go faster!*" I of course said, "*I don't need to go any faster!*"

2011 Annual Cruise

The destination for the Annual Cruise (AKA Commodore's Cruise) was decided by me as Sailing Secretary and proposed at the AGM in October.
There were several reasons for the decision to make Anstruther our destination:

1. It was somewhere different for a change; as a club we had never "cruised" the East Coast
2. There is an annual "Muster" at Anstruther, an organised weekend!
3. I wanted to incorporate a "Westerly Owners Muster" with our Cruise
4. It gave me a chance to catch up with all my old sailing buddies from the Forth.

The original plan was that I would compete in our own regatta on the 30th July and the cruise would leave the following morning heading for Whitehills.
Just after I had finalised all the details of the cruise, Lilly and I were invited to a wedding, in Perth, the same day as our regatta, which threw our plans up in the air.

The new plan was that I would attend the wedding with Lilly, then return from Perth early on the Sunday morning to arrive in Cromarty for midday where the other boats would wait for me then head off making our first stop Lossiemouth instead of the planned Whitehills;

This is an account of the trip:

Sunday 31st July 2011

I had worked out the passage plans for the trip and supplied each skipper with my planned waypoints and tide times etc, information which is required for passages such as we were about to undertake.

I arrived down at the Harbour at just after noon, *Willie Smeaton* ran me out to my mooring to bring my boat into the harbour where I could load all the "fresh produce" on board, the majority of the other gear of tinned food etc had already been loaded on board on the previous Wednesday.
"Octopus", owned and skippered by *Oliver Chapple,* with two of a crew, *Andrew Scott* and *Barry Devonald*, slipped their moorings as I was returning to the harbour.
The remaining three boats, *"Baccarat"*, owned and skippered by *Tom Paling* with *Bill Paterson* as crew, *"Moonshadow"*, (previously named *"Rusharound"*) owned and skippered by *Willie Smeaton,* with a crew of *Pete Loutit* and *"Heart of Gold"*, owned and skippered by me, *George Selvester,* with my trusty crew of *"Gingo" MacPhee* were casting off by 1245.

The winds were light and quite variable; we did manage a fair bit of sailing but resorted to some motor sailing to get into Lossiemouth Harbour at a reasonable time.

"Octopus" arrived at the port first closely followed by me in *"Heart of Gold"* and Willie with *"Moonshadow"* about ten minutes after me. Willie had touched the bottom on the way in which meant that Tom's boat with a draft of over 6ft would be unable to enter fully into the harbour, we caught his lines at the harbour mouth so that they could alight via the steps at the entrance and pulled his boat along the wall until it grounded. This was a tactic we had used with *"Moonshadow"* on an earlier visit.

Entrance to Lossiemouth Harbour

It was now out of the Swell and quite safe until the water, which, on the incoming tide, was already rising would be deep enough to pull it round and raft up to Willie's boat, this we managed to do within an hour of arrival.

I opened a box of red wine and invited all of the crews to join me in a celebration of the start of this years cruise.

The Skipper and Crew of "*Octopus*" then made their way up the "Ferry Boat" inn.

The other skippers and their crews organised the first evening meal, Gingo had prepared a Prawn Salad for him and me and Pete Loutit had prepared venison curry for his skipper and himself. We decided to share our "goodies" and made a sauce for the Prawns then rice to go with the curry and starters of Prawn Salad, as there was plenty to go round the crews of three boats had a very "classy" evening meal.

We also had copious amounts of wine before we too retired to the "Ferry Boat".

The pub was very quiet at first, which allowed us to sit and talk in a very convivial atmosphere. This was soon shattered by the arrival of a group of young men who seem to think that a pub needs loud music on to make it a pub!

I watched as three guys put a load of money into the "Juke Box" the with the music playing well above the safe level of decibels and could not believe that they themselves tried to conduct a conversation in impossible circumstances, we all left for the quiet and solitude of the boats. I then went to bed at a reasonable hour.

The trip from Cromarty had taken five hours.

Distance today: 26 Miles
Accumulative Distance: 26 Miles

Monday 1st August 2011.

The Harbourmaster made himself known to us around mid morning and promptly relieved us of £20 each for Harbour dues.

All the crews took advantage of the facilities here, excellent showers and toilets.

We had agreed to leave for Whitehills at 1230 and some of the crews took the opportunity of going up to the town for newspapers and other sundry items. By 1200 noon we were ready to go, except for *"Baccarat"* whose skipper and crew decided to say farewell to the barperson in the "Ferry Boat".

"Octopus" slipped her lines just after 1200 followed by *"Heart of Gold"* then *"Moonshadow"*, *"Baccarat"* would leave about twenty minutes after us but as she is the fastest boat will make up the ground on us in no time at all.

The trip to Whitehills was pretty uneventful, with conditions similar to those of yesterday; again we did some motor sailing to keep our cruise speed up.

Gingo got out the fishing rod at one point, seeing a lot of activity of gulls on the surface he decided there must be fish there, of course he was right and he managed to catch three mackerel.

As I had predicted earlier, "*Baccarat*" had caught us up and overhauled us leading the small fleet into Whitehills, the other three boats were tied up alongside by 1730.

When the harbourmaster came to me to collect the dues he said "I hear you are leaving at 0530 in the morning, I believe you have your tides back to front".

He suggested that we should leave no earlier than 0900, I had a long discussion with him regarding the tide flow at Rattray Head and although I had been confident with my initial plans, his comments put doubt in my mind.

I had the three mackerel for my supper, as Gingo likes catching fish but not eating them, before retiring to the pub.

The skippers and crew had a discussion at the pub later regarding the harbourmaster's comments and it was agreed that we could leave it a little later if we wanted.

After a few drinks we made our way back to the boats and into bed for the early rise.

Distance today: 27 Miles
Accumulative Distance: 53 Miles

Tuesday 2nd August 2011

Although the previous night's comments by Harbour Master had cast doubts in our minds everybody was up and raring to go at the time I had first stated, I checked my figures again and was convinced I was totally correct!

I think if I was sailing a large fishing vessel, which is what the harbourmaster had been doing for years I would not be quite so concerned about the hazard, however in our "little boats" it is imperative we get things right!
We set sail for Rattray head at 0530, one of the Dutch boats asked if he could join our little fleet to make the passage around the Head, I agreed and he left along with us. He even made his comments via channel 9 (our ship to ship communication) on the VHF.

There was a "misty" feel to the day and although visibility was limited, we could still see the land over two miles away on our starboard side. Willie contacted me again to ask if I was sure we were right and I said that if we were at *Kinnaird Head* at around 1000 we were spot on for the turn of the tide southwards at Rattray Head which is High Water Aberdeen -0420.

HW Aberdeen was 1610 BST this meant that the South Running Stream started at Rattray Head 1150

British SummerTime (1 hour ahead of Greenwich Mean time which is what tidal predictions are based on). I was extremely pleased when we were at the waypoint at almost the exact time I had predicted. There was a fair bit of turbulence with disturbed seas but nothing of any consequence and we sailed through this with little effort.

The Dutch yacht radioed us to thank us for our assistance and bade us farewell, as he was sailing onward to Eyemouth for his next port of call. I wished him good luck and we set our different courses.

From there to Peterhead is only 8 nautical miles and with the tidal assistance we covered this ground in around an hour and a half. I radioed Peterhead VTS asking for permission for four yachts travelling in company to enter the port.
He asked, in a broad Doric accent how far away from the entrance we were and if we were all together I confirmed that there was less than one hundred yards between the first and last boat and that at that time we were half a mile from the entrance. He instructed us to follow the supply ship in through the breakwater and remain on a listening watch on channel 14. By 1400 we were all inside the marina.

Gwyn Phillips, the Commodore, who had a hospital appointment in Raigmore, Inverness, for his broken arm on the Tuesday morning and had agreed to join us here, if he got the all clear from the hospital. True to his word he appeared at 1500. He would now be the other crewman for "*Baccarat*". "*Moonshadow*" still had a lot of venison which Pete had brought, so we had venison, which tasted more like roast beef, in a red wine sauce (made by Gingo) potatoes and vegetables.

After the meal the marina manager made an appearance and asked us for the dues for the night, my boat at 8 metres cost me £14 which is not bad at all considering there is electricity, water and showers available on single berth pontoons, unlike Cromarty where the charge is £20 for much less having no shower or toilet facilities.

We agreed to get a taxi into town, which is a good two miles from the marina, and thinking the Legion was open, this is where we headed. Unfortunately it does not open on a Tuesday night so we had to settle for the pub round the corner.

Our usual practise in cruises is that each boats stays with its own crew for the drinks but for some reason we ended up in one big round. This is not a good idea as the group then tend to drink at the rate of the fastest drinker and everyone ends up drinking too much too soon. That is my excuse for getting slightly tipsy and this coupled with the tiredness of a man my age I fell asleep in the chip shop.

I was told we had fish suppers before returning to the boat, I believe them ...I just don't remember!

Distance today: 41 Miles
Accumulative Distance: 94 Miles

Wednesday 3rd August 2011

When we rose in the morning the forecast had predicted fog and that is exactly what we got! We had visibility of around 50 yards but we were all quite confident that it would burn off as the sun got up. How wrong we were!

The little fleet was scheduled to depart this port at 1000. After showers/washes and breakfast it was all systems "GO". We contacted Peterhead VTS to request permission to leave the harbour. Nothing else was moving in the atrocious conditions, except of course, a bunch of half witted sailors, intent on achieving their goals!

"*Heart of Gold*" was first to leave the marina closely followed by "*Octopus*" then "*Moonshadow*". "*Baccarat*" had problems leaving as the water was so low (the bottom of the tide) that she touched bottom and had to wait half an hour before having sufficient water to sail out.
Once clear of the harbour mouth the next hazard was the "Skerry" a little island to the south east of

the harbour entrance I had set a course to miss it completely but with "*Moonshadow*" having a chart plotter I opted to follow him and told him of my intentions. Willie seemed to lose his bearings in the thick fog, even with the advantage of the chart plotter, and was virtually doing a 360-degree turn; "*Octopus*" could see what was happening and asked us via VHF what on earth we were doing.

I then decided that I could get myself into trouble so opted for my original plan of a clearing bearing on my own calculations. The fog cleared briefly allowing me to actually see the Skerry and to see "*Octopus*" on a heading straight for it! I quickly announced over the VHF for him to turn to port immediately and he did so averting a disaster!

Willie obviously went past without mishap and we continued on a southward course sailing completely blind and relying solely on the information from the GPS.

"*Baccarat*" then radioed to say that they were now leaving the harbour and all four boats were now on a course for Stonehaven. We sailed (or rather motored, as there was virtually no wind) for a couple of hours with no view of each other until at one waypoint, the Skares, I caught sight of "Octopus" about 25 yards to my starboard side, called him on the VHF to look to his port side and he then saw me. They then motored closer to us and together we made for the next waypoint. Oliver commented later that because we were all working from the same passage plan and waypoints list it was this reason he came upon us. It was comforting in the eerie fog to have another boat close to especially as he has radar!

All the boats communicated constantly on the VHF via Channel 9, "*Baccarat*" was following the same plan as "*Octopus*" and "*Heart of Gold*" but "*Moonshadow*" seemed to be working to his own plan. It turned out later that he had not programmed his chart plotter with the waypoints I had supplied before the cruise. This is something he rectified, once we reached Stonehaven.

Sailing in fog is not a nice experience and is very tiring. Every available pair of eyes must maintain a constant look out and your ears become your only radar. You also start to imagine things and at times are convinced that something is ahead of you.
At one point we came across a lone fisherman working his creel pots and we passed him without mishap.

My autohelm kept taking funny turns, suddenly veering off course and by the time I got it sorted out we had lost sight of "*Octopus*" again, he quickly found us again using his radar. This happened several times during the trip, which made good practise for Oliver and his crew in the use of radar. I still do not know what went wrong with the autohelm.

There is not a lot to report on the leg, because we could see absolutely nothing around us. At one point as we approached Aberdeen, I contacted VTS to tell them of the four yachts travelling in company but they treated this information with a total lack of interest, they did remark that we should be outside their VTS zone of three miles. I assured him our waypoints were outside the limits.
At one point *"Baccarat"* picked up a ship via AIS (Automatic Identification Systems) that was heading straight for us at a rate of 10 knots, Gwyn attempted to call them on 16 to warn them of our existence but got no reply, he then broadcast on 16 that they should be aware of the four yachts ahead of the ship and was promptly chastised via radio by MRCA that we should have used a working channel. That's logic for you... some twit putting protocol before safety!

By 1700 both *"Octopus"* and *"Heart of Gold"* arrived at the waypoint for the entrance to Stonehaven and we were most surprised to see *"Baccarat"* looming out of the fog ahead of us, we firmly believed he was still behind us, all three yachts headed into this fine little harbour with perfect safety, a great sense of relief at having got here without any incidents.

I rafted alongside Oliver with Westerly Centaur on the outside of me. Fifteen minutes later, Willie appeared through the fog and rafted up against *"Baccarat".*

Gingo went ashore in search of a shop to buy some supplies we had run out of, kitchen roll, and when he came back he had bought some fresh fish and some smoked fish and set about making Cullen Skink for our supper.

Pete Loutit had also gone foraging and returned with a lobster and two crabs, he then realised he had not a pot big enough to boil them so went back ashore to buy one. Tom Paling bought steaks for supper which he intended barbequing, we again decided to share the food we had and we all sat on *"Baccarat"* to eat a perfect meal of Cullen Skink, followed by lobster and crab salad then barbequed steaks, washed down of course with copious amounts of wine.

At that point I had a feeling that I may well return home with a bad case of Gout from all this rich living!

We did sample the local hostelry before retiring to bed after a very tiring day.

Distance today: 35 Miles
Accumulative Distance: 129 Miles

Thursday 4th August 2011.

I had ran out of gas (yet again!) and went in search of a supplier, it turned out the nearest stockist was several miles away and Gingo and I set off on foot to get it with the empty gas bottle in hand, after less than half a mile my old ankles began giving me great discomfort, when suddenly a man stopped us and said *"you are obviously looking for the gas supplier which is a good distance away would you like me to run you there, my car is just over here"?*
Somewhere in my youth and childhood, I must have done something good!

The fog today was even worse than yesterday and I said that there was no way I was doing the same again, this is supposed to be a holiday and I am not into self flagellation! Willie agreed with me then the vote came down on remaining put till the fog clears. We used the day cleaning the boats getting more diesel and of course, a trip to the local pubs

Distance today: 0 Miles
Accumulative Distance: 129 Miles

Friday 5th August 2011.

A quick skippers meeting after breakfast and we decided we would leave here two hours before the flood tide which meant leaving at 1000 and having to stem the tide for over two hours, with very little wind, it meant motor sailing again in an effort to maintain our cruising speed.

Even with the motor on we were only managing 3.5 knots over the ground and the GPS was telling us our *estimated time of arrival* was very late indeed.

When the tide did turn we got a little more wind and a great help from the flood of the spring tide and at some points were achieving a very respectable 7 knots over the ground without the motor.

Jock Wingate phoned me to ask what time we expected to be in Anstruther as he and Robert Hogg were driving down to join us; I said that I expected to be in well after 2000.

The wind was not quite "on the nose" but it made a challenge to sail as close to our course as we could, "*Baccarat*" at one point thought it would be better to sail to the seaward side of the Bell Rock Lighthouse (twelve miles offshore) and tack back in, I preferred the other option of going more toward the shore, then tacking back out.

Luckily for all concerned, there was a little wind shift and we managed to sail almost perfectly on course from Bell Rock to the cardinal mark at North Carr. When we were 1.5 M north of the cardinal mark I phoned Donald Thomson, with whom I sailed for many years on the Firth of Forth, I had arranged to meet him and some other old friends at Anstruther to let him know when we would be in.

On arrival at the cardinal mark we were still sailing, but as we approached Fife Ness, the wind turned further round to the west and was now directly in our face, I started the motor again, by now I was desperate to get into harbour!

Willie Smeaton called on the radio, to let us know he was having engine problems and that he would probably need a tow. "*Octopus*" obliged, but in the conditions her engine started to overheat, and had to let go of the tow. Willie had no option but to ask for assistance from the Coastguard who sent the lifeboat out to him.

I was really surprised at the amount of creel markers in this area, I do not exaggerate when I say there were thousands; I cannot understand how this can be sustainable!

The last few miles as always seem to take the longest time, but eventually the breakwater became closer and closer until at last we entered the harbour at 1945. I travelled through the outer harbour and as I entered the inner harbour I spotted Donald's Boat, "*Quintaine*" a Cobra 28ft, and rafted up alongside him. He came on deck to greet us and to offer us a celebratory drink for our arrival, judging by his speech and the rolling eyes he had been celebrating most of the day!

Jock Wingate and Robert Hogg were on the dockside and as soon as I was tied up Jock came aboard bearing gifts of a bottle of Black Bottle Whisky and a bottle of red wine. As Donald was on his boat alone, we came to an arrangement that Jock could have a berth for the night aboard *"Quintaine"*.

"Heart of Gold" alongside *"Quintaine"* in Anstruther

"Baccarat" and *"Octopus"* followed us into the harbour within half an hour, then came Willie's spectacular entrance behind the lifeboat. Willie was

to tell me later, that they were towed at 9 knots on the way in!

"Moonshadow" being rescued

The partying in the big marquee, which had been erected for the "Weekend Muster", was already in full swing and the noise from the music and merriment inside the tent drifted across the harbour in the now still airs of the night.

Donald then set about making a chicken curry and rice for Jock, Gingo, me and him, after scoffing this down we set about the bottles Jock had brought, I am not a whisky drinker, but Jock and Donald managed to empty ¾ of the bottle at one sitting. I had a couple of glasses of wine but I was not feeling too great and was also very tired, so just wanted to go to bed. I eventually managed to tear myself away at 2300 and slipped into my sleeping bag for a good night's rest.

Distance today: 51 Miles
Accumulative Distance: 180 Miles

Saturday 6th August 2011.

On Robert's arrival aboard *"Moonshadow"*, he was given the task of sorting out the problems with Willie's engine. Saturday morning saw him scurrying back and forth from the Harbourmaster's Office having had the workshop manual for the engine downloaded from the computer. He returned several times in search of special tools and pullers all of which seemed too readily available in and around the various shops and workshops dotted around this harbour.

After breakfast and a shower and payment of my harbour dues we sat aboard Donald's boat and reminisced of days gone by, before we knew it the pubs were open so we had to sample the local hospitality. There was a memorial service held for the lives lost on two submarines, which collided in poor visibility off the Isle of May in 1918. Gingo spoke to a couple of serving officers from today's submarine fleet telling them that his son Graham is serving as a chief on submarines at Faslane.

To learn more of the fate of the said submarines, visit:
http://en.wikipedia.org/wiki/Battle_of_May_Island

We only had a couple of pints of lager, then went to visit Scott McConnachie aboard his 36 foot American ketch, "*Zeye*", where we were treated to a couple of cans of lager and hot sausage rolls for lunch.
I continued the stories of days gone by with Scott, Donald and Joe McCrystal, with all of whom I had spent many happy years sailing at Blackness Boat Club on the upper reaches of the Forth.

I had already told many stories to my current sailing buddies of times we had, but I must admit I left out some of the embarrassing stories, if I thought that the Three Amigos were going to keep quiet about them, I was sadly mistaken. All the stories came out, "warts and all", but it was all in good fun.

I received a phone call from my son, Steve and my daughter-in-law Teleri, to let me know that they were heading in my direction from Edinburgh with my granddaughter, Rowan, who at eight months old I had yet to meet.

They duly arrived at 1700 and we drove to the village of Crail to have a meal together. It was great to see Rowan, she is such a good natured baby, I would have loved to have spent more time with them, but they needed to get back to Edinburgh, and I was due to be at the tent for 1900 for the prize giving. I was also still feeling a little under the weather.

Lilly and I had already arranged to go down to Wales for a weekend in September so we could spend more quality time with them then.

Steve ran me back to the tent for 1900 and we said our farewells, on entering the tent there was not any of our lot there so I went looking for them on Scott's boat, sure enough there they were drinking more wine.

We made our way to the tent and the band was in full swing we pushed some tables together to accommodate our crowd and had a couple of drinks before the prize giving started.

There are several prizes awarded, best dressed boat is one prize and the most travelled boat to the event is another, this is usually awarded to a single boat, but as all four of our boats had the same mileage, which was the highest, we were awarded the prize as a club.

On collecting the prize and having the mandatory pictures taken I decided that I was too unwell to enjoy anymore of the festivities and made my way back to the boat and into bed by 2000.

We collected the Prize for furthest travelled

Gingo was to tell me in the morning, that he said to the rest of the skippers and crews that he was worried that I might die on the way home and he would not know what to do. Apparently a discussion then ensued about whether the radio call made should be a "Pan-Pan" or a "Mayday". John Carson said it should be a "Mayday" for a dead skipper, it was not very comforting to find out they were more concerned for his welfare than mine!

Distance today: 0 Miles
Accumulative Distance: 180 Miles

Sunday 7th August 2011.

The weather forecast for this day was bleak with strong Northerly winds, which would suit Scott and Donald, as they would be "reaching" up the Forth to their home port of Queensferry.
Around 1100 they set off and we bade them fair winds and good sailing. Our group have decided to wait another day to see what that forecast brings.

I had moved "*Heart of Gold*" across the harbour to let Donald away and I was now rafted up to "*Baccarat*" where we would stay until we sailed for home.
We made our way up to " The Bank" pub because it has wi-fi and with Gwyn's laptop tried to get the synoptic charts to get a better idea of the weather patterns affecting us.

Some of the guys had a pub lunch when here but Gingo and I opted to eat later on board. The weather outlook was not good it indicated we would have the northerly winds for the following 24 hours.

We sat and chatted away in the pub for a while then returned to the boat for a meal, we would meet up later in the Salutation pub for a little party, there being little else to do in this town.

We had to shift back a little to let the *"Reaper"* into her own berth. She had been moved to Pittenweem, to make room for all the visiting yachts at the muster.
Again I was early to bed.

Distance today: 0 Miles
Accumulative Distance: 180 Miles

"Heart of Gold" rafted to "Baccarat"

Monday 8th August 2011.

Weather had worsened and we could be here for a lot longer than we anticipated, winds still in the north and getting stronger, welcome to the *Cromarty Boat Club Cruise*..Wherever we are going is where the wind is coming from.

After breakfast and ablutions, some of the other crews decided to walk from Anstruther to Pittenweem, over a mile to the west of us. As Gingo and myself have bad legs and ankles, we have difficulty walking any further than the pub, which is exactly what we did. We bought some newspapers and sat and read them, Gingo went to the bookies to put on a couple of bets. Pete Loutit and Bill Paterson appeared and we sat and talked of many things;

of shoes and ships and sealing wax, of cabbages and kings.

(Unless the reader is acquainted with Lewis Carroll quotations this will mean nothing to them!)

We did have a wander round the RNLI shop but saw nothing we actually wanted to buy.
The others had now returned from their walk and we visited "The Bank" pub again to get a weather update for Tuesday. At last things are looking up. Easterlies are forecast for Tuesday morning, we should be able to leave in the morning.

During the day the boats had taken the opportunity of cleaning and replenishing water stocks etc, "*Octopus*" had left its berth to take up a position on the pontoons to take on water, the wind was making it difficult to moor as the boat was taking a fair bit of windage, the boat, now sitting with its bow on the pontoon was having difficulty getting a line ashore, skipper Oliver yelled to crewman Andrew "Jump!" and like a true military man Andrew jumped into the harbour!

Later in the pub he would tell us that it was done because the gas bottle in the lifejacket was out of date! Aye! Whatever Andrew! He was soon pulled clear and no one came to any harm.

Pete Loutit had wanted to sail with us to Stonehaven today and his wife Jean (who was visiting their daughter in Banchory) would have picked him up from there, this is now up in the air by us being weather-bound again: *the best laid plans of mice and men gang aft aglay* (Robert Burns this time!).

Jean phoned to say that she had arrived and as we went back to the pub again we saw them drive off. I can't recall what we did for the rest of the day, I thought this was a cute little town when we sailed in but I now feel like a prisoner and I am desperate to escape from the place!

I do recall quite a convivial night in the Salutation bar where all the crews mustered and listened to

Gingo regaling some of his "worth listening to" stories, the banter and humour between all of us was very entertaining.

We discussed the plans for the morning and it was agreed that we would leave as soon as we had sufficient water under our keels, this decision having been made, I returned to the boat and the comfort of my bunk.

Distance today: 0 Miles
Accumulative Distance: 180 Miles

Tuesday 9th August 2011.

Gingo and I were up washed and fed by 0630 and ready to cast off. I looked into Baccarat to see what state of readiness they had reached and was told by Gwyn, who was still inside his sleeping bag, to "Piss Off"! That is exactly what we did. As we sailed past "*Moonshadow*" and "*Octopus*" I called to say we were on our way. Willie came back to me via channel 9 to say he would be at least half an hour getting out, as they did not quite have enough water yet. "*Heart of Gold*" cleared the harbour confines by 0700 and headed eastward for the open sea.

We were only out about ten minutes when we received a call on the VHF from Oliver saying that he was now having problems with his starter motor and that Bill Paterson was on his way over from *"Baccarat"* to have a look at it. Willie and Robert managed to get out about twenty minutes after us and were now following us toward the cardinal mark at North Carr.

Once we rounded Fife Ness the wind was good and strong and from a decent direction of just south of east we were making a good 6.5 knots over the ground even against the tide. The tide would turn in our favour until 1230-1300 but it is neaps and not as crucial as it was on the southbound journey. It seemed to be no time at all until we were approaching Bell Rock, we received news from *"Baccarat"*, who was now two hours behind us that Oliver's starter motor is "duff" and they were waiting for an engineer to determine whether or not they require it to be repaired or indeed a complete new motor.

The next call we got from *"Baccarat"* was to tell us they were 5 miles south of the Bell Rock and I replied that we were the same distance to the north.

Soon after that the wind started to drop and move more to NE, I decided to start motoring again, this is a long leg and it is very tiring for anyone let alone a 68 year old. I know that Francis Chichester did a circumnavigation of the world in his 66th year, but I am not that keen! I wanted into Stonehaven as quickly as I could.

Another VHF Communication from Willie, told us that he was having trouble with his engine again; I said that in the conditions, a big swell of 2 metres, I could not possibly take him in tow. They had no alternative but to continue sailing. The remainder of the trip from there to Stonehaven was boring and Gingo had to put up with my moaning all the way there.

We sailed into Stonehaven harbour for the second time in a week and tied up by 1700. I had a shower and on my return to the boat I cooked a quick meal of pasta and meat for Gingo and myself whilst he went for a shower.

By the time we had eaten and washed the dishes, "*Baccarat*" was calling us from about a mile away Gwyn asked me what the swell was like at the harbour entrance and I assured him it was fine. Stonehaven is bad for entry in an easterly swell. They entered the harbour at 1930 with "*Moonshadow*" limping in thirty minutes later.

A text message from Oliver, confirmed that their starter was indeed dead and they had to wait for a replacement, which would not arrive until lunchtime on Wednesday.

The crews of the other two boats, opted for a pub meal but had to hurry to beat the deadline of the chef going home. Gingo and I joined them and had a drink, everyone was tired after the long day and it was back to the boats by 2200.

Distance today: 51 Miles
Accumulative Distance: 231 Miles

Wednesday 10th August 2011.

And then there were two!

Willie has made the decision to have his boat lifted out and transported by road to Inverness where he can work on the engine at his leisure over the next couple of months.

Wind was from the east again and is considerably stronger than the previous day but would ensure that we could make good progress to Peterhead, the remaining two boats left the harbour together at 1000. The swell was quite big but once clear of the harbour, we got the sails up and settled down for a roller coaster ride all the way to Peterhead.
We still had two hours plus of tide against us but the sailing was good and we were making excellent time.

The rain was incessant and in no time at all I could feel it penetrating my now quite elderly "Musto" gear, the visibility was down a fair bit due to the unbelievable rain and with the seas becoming even bigger, as the wind increased it was very uncomfortable trying to sit in a decent position. I did not want to complain too much, as this was the fastest we had been sailing during the whole time away.

Again we used a waypoint well outside the VTS are for Aberdeen, there was another yacht that had left Stonehaven just after us but they were sailing closer into the land than us.

Steadily over the day, "*Baccarat*" pulled further and further ahead of us until just before the Buchan Ness Light came into view, when they disappeared from completely from my sight.

As I sailed passed the Skerry, the other yacht on passage called VTS from Buchan Ness asking for permission to enter the harbour, I then called for permission and when asked my position told him we were off the Skerry, he gave us the green light to enter and as Gingo took down the sails, we motored into the relative calm of the harbour then on into the flat calm of the marina. The time was now 1745.

Gwyn gave us a shout to join them, on "*Baccarat*", as they had the central heating system running; we entered the warmth of their cabin and had a couple of drinks with them. Gingo went back to our boat and prepared a big casserole, whilst Tom prepared more potatoes and together we enjoyed a hot meal. Tom also produced another bottle of wine and we sat and talked for an hour or so, but with some of my clothes still a little damp, I was finding it difficult to warm up, I made my excuses and again sought the comfort of my sleeping bag.

Contact again from "*Octopus*", indicated that they were on their way again having left Anstruther at 1300; they planned to sail to Peterhead in one hop and were achieving a steady 6.5 knots, I estimate they should get here at round 0330 if the winds would continue.
A tiring though worthwhile day, I was in bed by 2200.

Distance today: 35 Miles
Accumulative Distance: 266 Miles

Thursday 11th August 2011.

Now we were three again!

"*Octopus*" had arrived during the night; I walked up to the toilet block and by the time I returned, Gingo had started making the breakfast.
Having studied the tides again for rounding Rattray Head, Gwyn, Tom and I agreed we should leave here

at 1300 to arrive at Rattray head by 1500, as the north running stream starts Aberdeen High Water +0140.
All the boats in the marina had wet weather gear hanging from every line and stay, to dry them off in the morning sun and early breeze.

"Octopus" early morning in Peterhead

Having plenty time before we leave I went for a shower and paid my harbour dues. On returning to the boat, Oliver was up and about from "*Octopus*" and enquired what time we planned leaving here. I gave him the information he requested and he went off to waken his crew.

I was to learn that they were apparently off the harbour mouth by 0400 but they were reluctant to enter in darkness and waited for first light, which was around 0500.

They did a fantastic job of sailing overnight in what were very trying conditions. Well done lads!

The small fleet sailed out at the agreed time of 1300 after receiving clearance from Peterhead harbour radio; we all hoisted our mainsails in the relative calm of the harbour before pushing out into a huge swell of the harbour mouth.

There is a reef runs out eastward about a half mile north of the harbour entrance and as the tide swirls round this reef the seas become very disturbed. The wave height for the short period of time is about 5 metres and the boats get tossed around like rubber ducks!!

Once clear of this disturbed area we could settle down for a fairly decent sail, the easterly swell of around 2 metres was still a bit uncomfortable but bearable and the regular rhythm makes it easy to adjust yourself to it.
We were making about 6 knots under sail, which was quite pleasing, and arrival at the waypoint was almost exactly what we wanted. There was a little bit of disturbance with the tide, but nothing we could not cope with.

By the time we reached the next waypoint off Kinnaird Head, the wind had dropped again quite considerably, Oliver radioed and said they were going to motor, we followed suit. From that point to Whitehills was relative boring, apart from the fact that the coastguard helicopter was searching for an EPIRB (Electronic Positioning Indicating Radio Beacon) signal somewhere off Pennan Head and MCA were making radio calls trying to determine the source.

We arrived at Whitehills by 1945 and there was a mad scramble to get to the local chip shop before it stopped serving at 2030, with everyone now armed with a fish supper and a glass of wine, courtesy of "*Octopus*", we sat down to enjoy our meal.

"Heart of Gold" entering Whitehills

I wandered up to the local pub with Oliver and his crew, whilst the others stayed onboard. We only had two drinks in the bar then walked back down to the boats. Oliver and I agreed that it would be in the best interest of both boats to make an early start at 0500, Gwyn and Tom and Bill said they would wait until closer to 0900.

I had one last drink aboard "*Baccarat*" before retiring at 2300.

Distance today: 41 Miles
Accumulative Distance: 307 Miles

Friday 12th August 2011.

Gingo woke me at 0430, at first I did not feel like getting up and looking at the harbour entrance I felt there was not enough water. I lay back down on my bunk for about 20 minutes then I heard familiar throb of the engine of Olivers boat as he motored out of the harbour, if he can get out, so can I!

We followed soon after and once clear of the waypoint, turned for home. We received a message via VHF thanking us for our company over the two weeks and a promise that they would join us again next year, with that they opened up the throttle and slowly pulled away from us.

The wind was from the south and gave us a little drive but with the mileage we had to do today, I kept the engine going to give us 6+knots.

After we passed Lossiemouth the wind picked up considerably and we managed 7 knots without the engine, this kept up until we were about 10 miles from the Sutors so the engine was back on, now desperate to get home again.
The wind had come right round to the west but only lasted around 20 minutes before dropping away to nothing.

Under power for the remainder of the trip we passed the Buss Bank Buoy at 1245 and tied up alongside the harbour wall at 1330.

It was nice to be back home, and I was so happy that we had achieved all we set out to do for the first cruise in many years.

I thank all those who took part in the cruise and look forward sailing with them again in the near future.

Distance today: 41 Miles
Accumulative Distance: 360 Miles

Last Event of the season

Gingo acted as crew for me again in the last event of the 2011 season, the Black Isle Challenge Cup.
This event has a social gathering afterwards at which the prizes for the MYA series are awarded; it is a very good event to mark the end of the season.

I picked up my prizes won in the MYA series and the Club were awarded third place in the group section. The race itself however was a bit of a disaster with my personal performance pretty poor. It is easy to make excuses that the boat did not have a "clean" underwater hull which did slow us down.

However, I made several mistakes, one being that I tacked too early before Chanonry point and came very close to the shore. I was reluctant to put in another tack as it would mean losing too much ground. I sailed with my fingers crossed that we would not touch the bank and sailed within feet of the shore; I did hear the port keel scrape through the sand as I passed the point.

I also made a complete hash of flying the spinnaker and lost even more ground during that fiasco.
I cannot blame the boat, for as we have already established:

"It's the sailor, not the boat"

"Heart of Gold" scrapes past the point!

"Heart of Gold" messes up with the spinnaker and Fram cashes in by stealing a march on my mistake

I am now almost 69 years of age but my mind thinks I am 29, pity I can't convince my body to believe it!

I am hoping to sail for another 52 years but perhaps I am being just a trifle optimistic!

George Selvester March 2012